LONGMAN RESOURCES
FOR WRITERS

LEARNING TOGETHER

An Introduction to Collaborative Learning

*T*ori Haring-Smith

Brown University

LONGMAN

An imprint of Addison Wesley Longman, Inc.

New York • Reading, Massachusetts • Menlo Park, California • Harlow, England
Don Mills, Ontario • Sydney • Mexico City • Madrid • Amsterdam

Senior Editor: Jane Kinney
Project Editor: Ellen MacElree
Design Supervisor/Modified Text Design: Wendy Ann Fredericks
Cover Design: John Callahan
Production Administrator: Linda Murray
Compositor: Digitype, Inc.
Printer and Binder: R. R. Donnelley & Sons Company
Cover Printer: New England Book Components, Inc.

Learning Together: An Introduction to Collaborative Learning

Library of Congress Cataloging-in-Publication Data

Haring-Smith, Tori.
    Learning together : an introduction to collaborative learning /
Tori Haring-Smith.
        p.   cm. — (Longman resources for writers)
    Includes index.
    ISBN 0-673-46848-8
    1. Group work in education.   2. Team learning approach in
education.   3. Authorship—Collaboration.   I. Title.
LB1032.H37   1993
371.1'02—dc20   92-31795
                                                                              CIP

Acknowledgments
Outlines on pp. 22–23 and 30–31: Excerpts from *Women's Ways of Knowing* by Mary Field Belenky et al. Copyright © 1986 by Basic Books, Inc. Reprinted by permission of Basic Books, a division of HarperCollins Publishers Inc.
Dialogues on pp. 47 and 62: From *Sharing Writing* by Karen Spear (Boynton/Cook Publishers, Portsmouth, NH, 1988). Reprinted by permission of Karen Spear.
Cartoon on p. 94: The Far Side cartoon by Gary Larson is reprinted by permission of Chronicle Features, San Francisco. Copyright © 1984.

    99 00 01 9 8 7 6

CONTENTS

PREFACE

Our society promotes the myth of the individual achiever. In school, we learn about the accomplishments of great people like George Washington Carver, Virginia Woolf, and Copernicus. But in fact, none of these people worked in isolation. Their achievements were the result of group effort — of collaboration. Recent studies have shown that human beings do their best work when they work together. Unfortunately, our schools teach students to work in isolation from one another. Students are told to "do their own work" and are tested solely on their performance as individuals. Our cultural myths and educational practices, then, do not reflect the way real people solve real problems.

Interest in how people work together is growing in all fields. Business schools are promoting collaborative management skills, psychologists are studying "ensemble individualism," and medical schools are teaching students to determine diagnoses as a group. Even the 1992 Earth Summit in Rio de Janeiro reflected our growing sense that countries must collaborate to address the problems of our deteriorating environment.

There is also a growing movement to change the way that Americans are taught. Why should we teach students to work alone in classrooms and then expect them to work in groups on the job? Teachers who use collaborative learning are trying to improve this situation. They want to teach their students to work in groups as well as alone. But adopting new classroom practices is never easy, and this change is particularly difficult because it redefines the roles of both teacher and student. Students must learn not only by listening to the teacher but also by listening to each other and sharing ideas. In this way, they discover knowledge rather than just absorb it. They become active learners. Teachers must also change what they do in order to achieve a collaborative classroom. They must learn to step aside and let the students do some of the learning for themselves. They cannot just digest information and feed it to students — they must establish an environment in which the students can discover knowledge for themselves.

This book is addressed to both teachers and students who want to try collaborative learning. It could be used by colleges, graduate programs, or professional schools and is designed to help students on assignments in any field — science, social science, humanities, arts, business, or professional studies. On-the-job training programs may also find it useful. Chapter 1 defines collaborative learning in greater depth than this brief preface can. Chapter 2 explains how groups work together best and what special problems they must learn to overcome. The last two chapters discuss the most common kind of collaborative assignment — writing together.

I have been using collaborative learning in my classroom for a decade and have led over one hundred workshops on the subject at colleges, universities, and businesses. This book is the culmination of that experience. I am greatly indebted to all the participants in my workshops who have helped me understand how collaborative learning can be used as part of a traditional classroom or on its own. In addition, I am grateful to the following individuals for their reviews of the manuscript: Chris Amirault, University of Wisconsin at Milwaukee; Karen Spear, Fort Lewis College; and John Trimbur, Worcester Polytechnic Institute. Other colleagues who have spoken to me through their letters and from the pages of their own books include Peter Elbow, Lisa Ede, Alfie Kohn, Andrea Lunsford, Blythe Clinchy, Ken Bruffee, Harvey Kail, Tom Blackburn, Margot Soven, and Barbara Sylvester. Students who have taken my courses and served as Writing Fellows in our cross-curricular writing program have given me the students' perspective on collaboration. They have tested my theories and guided my thinking.

I originally decided to write this book for Carolyn Potts, then an editor at Little, Brown, and her inspiration was invaluable. Since then, the efforts of Constance Rajala, Anne Smith, Jane Kinney, Ellen MacElree, and Rosemary Wellner at Longman have seen the book to its completion.

My family has also been very supportive. My mother, an archivist, spends her time organizing material so that she can help others learn about history, technology, anthropology, music, and literature. My father, a college professor for over twenty-five years, got me interested in teaching. In presiding over dinner-table conversations, he exemplifies the arts of intellectual discussion and careful listening. Finally, I want to thank my husband and my son who have seen me through the ordeal of writing this manuscript. They have given an entirely new meaning to the phrase "learning together." My husband sacrificed many weekends so that I could sit at the computer, and my son learned to play by himself while I worked, an odd side effect of a book that focuses on togetherness and support.

Tori Haring-Smith

CHAPTER
1

WHAT IS COLLABORATIVE LEARNING?

We work together, whether together or apart.

Robert Frost

When you think of great inventors, national leaders, and famous writers, what do you visualize? Do you see a solitary individual like Albert Einstein hunched over his calculations, scribbling away? Do you imagine Emily Dickinson sitting alone in an attic room? Or, do you see people working together — the early leaders of this country huddled together in candlelight, piecing together a manifesto for a new nation? Do you see a famous novelist like Hemingway talking about a new book with his editor?

Although our historical and cultural mythology encourages us to think of great ideas, discoveries, and events as the product of individual effort, in fact they usually result from group effort. We remember Alexander Graham Bell and his telephone, Marie Curie and radium, Aristotle and the definition of tragedy, or Martin Luther King and the civil rights movement. But none of these people worked alone. Bell developed his invention with his associate, Thomas Watson; Curie performed most of her experiments with her husband or her daughter; Aristotle spent twenty years discussing ideas with thinkers in Plato's Academy and later with his friend Theophrastus; and Martin Luther King had a small army of supporters surrounding him as he marched out of Selma. There are, of course, hermits and solitary geniuses in our society, but they are the exceptions — so exceptional, in fact, that we frequently brand them peculiar or even insane.

It is not surprising, then, that recent research in education, psychology, and business management shows us that people can accomplish more if they work together. Dozens of studies have revealed that people working as a group to solve mazes or number puzzles can outperform individuals working alone at the same task. And perhaps the most interesting research demonstrates that groups even solve puzzles more accurately than the brightest individual in them could alone.

The myth of the isolated individual achiever has strongly influenced the way in which we teach students at all levels in America. Only the youngest students are encouraged to share ideas and rely on one another as they work. Our schools devote far more time to judging individual performance than to encouraging students to learn by working together. In this way, traditional education has failed to model the way real progress is accomplished. It is little wonder that we speak of school as an ivory tower distinguished from the so-called "real world." Work is accomplished in different ways in those two worlds.

To see how much this thinking has pervaded your own assumptions, picture students who are learning. What do you see? Do you see a classroom filled with rows and rows of teenagers silently bending over their notebooks taking down lecture notes? Do you see a solitary person reading in the library? Or, do you see groups of students working together to understand the complexities of contract law or macroeconomics? Do you imagine heated discussions in the cafeteria or a pair of people working on a lab experiment?

This book is designed to help you work together as students. Most people think that students are isolated individuals who compete for a limited number of A's and so must avoid sharing their ideas. Many students believe that they must work alone because working together — collaborating — is the same as cheating. The word does have a double connotation. In my *American Heritage Dictionary*, for example, the two meanings of *collaborate* are:

1. To work together, especially in a joint intellectual effort.
2. To cooperate treasonably, as with an enemy occupying one's country.

These definitions show us that working together can be either a positive or negative idea. The first definition reflects the way that I will use the word *collaboration* in this book. But look at the second definition of *collaboration*. If sharing ideas in school is collaboration in that sense of the word, then the metaphor implies that we invade each other's mental countries when we share ideas. I remember that the honor code in my high school presented this view of collaborating and forbade students from working together. Unfortunately, most students accept this battle metaphor and carefully guard their ideas from any spies. For them, collaboration is a crime.

Well, if people outside school were punished for collaborating, most of our society would be paying fines every day. If they could not collaborate, how would lawyers within a firm share information about an important case? How would working mothers manage to do their jobs and raise their children? How well would a basketball team succeed if the players were more interested in showing off their individual talents than in working together as a team? How would medical researchers share important discoveries in order to develop a cure for cancer? Of course, this book does not advocate plagiarism or cheating. There are times when your teacher will want you to work alone, and you must respect these instructions. Adopting someone else's idea and calling it your own is always wrong. But developing ideas as a group member or in response to someone else's work is quite natural. This distinction will become clearer as we discuss specific ways of working together.

LEARNING TOGETHER

Because the exercises in this book ask you to share ideas and learn together in a particular way, I want to explain how collaborative learning is different from many other kinds of learning. Collaborative learning is going to ask you to be a different kind of student than you may have been in the past. It redefines your relationship to your teacher and to the other students in your class. Instead of assuming that class is a time when you can sit back and be told about the history of South Africa, the functions of the kidney, or the "rules" for good prose, this book suggests that you can learn by doing as well as by listening.

The classroom in which collaborative learning is used looks quite different from a more traditional lecture or class discussion. You will work in pairs or small groups, you may move about the room rather than sit still, and you will find out answers for yourselves rather than waiting for the teacher to give you the answer. In fact, in most of these exercises, there is no "right answer," so you and your groups will be developing and defending your own ideas, not just trying to figure out "what the teacher wants."

Have you been asked to work in groups before and thought, "What a waste of time. Why doesn't the teacher just lecture?" Have you ever waited patiently through a class discussion in order to find out what the teacher really thinks? If you have been asked to read and comment on another student's paper, have you wondered what you could possibly have to say? Or, maybe most of your teachers have spent class time presenting material to you, while you took notes or worked on homework.

If any of these experiences sounds familiar, you will find collaborative learning a new approach. Of course, it is not a new kind of learning — in fact, reading, talking, and learning together was the practice in most schools until the twentieth century. But collaborative learning is not very common in American schools now. The first rules that most students learn in school are

- Be quiet.
- Don't talk to other students.
- Do your own work.

Our school systems have become so concerned with testing individual comprehension of material that they have stopped students from learning together. This has had a very serious effect on how well students learn, and it has warped our assumptions about teachers' and students' roles in the classroom. Let's look at how collaborative learning challenges the kind of schooling most Americans now receive.

In order to work together with your classmates, you will have to recognize the knowledge and experience that you and your classmates have. Why work with others if you don't think that they have anything worthwhile to share? Why ask someone to respond to your writing if you think that only the teacher can do that? Most students have gradually come to distrust the knowledge that they and their classmates have. The American educational system teaches most students that they should listen to the teacher, memorize what she and the textbooks say, and then regurgitate that information on exams and in papers. In many cases, students find it easier to forget or ignore what they think and just concentrate on what the teacher thinks.

I know that when I was a student, I was often afraid to speak in class. It seemed safer to be quiet than to be wrong. I remember sitting in English class and thinking, "Where did the teacher get that interpretation of this text? I thought that the poem was about a flower and she says that it is about existentialism." I learned to keep quiet rather than reveal my ignorance. I think many students share my fear of being wrong. Consequently, it is not surprising that American educators today bemoan the fact that their students are passive.

I had forgotten about this trick of being a student until one day when I was teaching "The Thorn," a poem by William Wordsworth, to a class on Romantic Literature. I was explaining how funny the poem was, and the students were nodding and writing down, "The poem is funny." If asked on an exam to comment on this poem, they would probably say that the poem was funny. At the time, it did not seem at all odd to me that undoubtedly none of them laughed when they read the poem and none were laughing now as I explained how funny the poem was. I would not have thought much about this if a student in the class had not raised her hand and asked me the best question I have ever been asked by a student. She said, "If you were not an English teacher, how would you know that this poem is funny?"

Suddenly I realized something important: by ignoring the fact that my students did not necessarily come to class thinking that "The Thorn" was a funny poem, I was not really teaching them to read poetry. I was simply asking them to accept and remember my reading of the poem (which, by the way, I received from a professor who told me that the poem was funny). I really *do* think that the poem is funny, but I was not showing my students how to see the poem that way. I was simply seeing it that way for them. I was performing for them, and they were passively watching and taking notes.

In most colleges and universities, teachers and students alike assume that students are empty vessels, waiting to be filled with the knowledge of calculus, Chinese history, modern American architecture, or whatever. The basic definition of a teacher is one who knows a subject, while a student is assumed to be ignorant of the subject. Now to some extent, this is true. You take a class in organic chemistry because you want to learn organic chemistry. If you already knew the subject, you would probably try to "test out" of the course and take a different one. Of course, you might take a diagnostic test at the beginning of a course to see how much American history or calculus you remember, but these random questions can't really tell teachers what you know about a subject. If you know that Washington was president before Lincoln, does this mean that you also understand the different cultural or political climates in which these two men worked? If you write, "IF $3A + 2 = 8$, THEN A = 2," how will the teacher know if you made a lucky guess, knew the answer intuitively, or really understand how to work algebra problems?

Most of the time, you do know something about the subject of the courses you take. Your courses up to this point have prepared you for organic chemistry. You have learned methods for balancing chemical equations, and you understand the basic structure of chemical compounds. Similarly, although you may never have taken a course in Chinese history, you probably know something about it — that it involves many dynasties, that China was a great silk producer, that Chinese women used to bind their feet, that the Chinese built the Great Wall, that the Communist party has been crushing political dissent, and so on. Some of the things that you "know" about a subject may not be "true." For example, based on popular media, you might assume that the Chinese were especially ruthless warriors. You might also have memorized incorrect valences for certain chemical elements. In any case, your mind is not a blank slate.

Not only do you come into a course with knowledge and experience that is relevant to it, but, as you go along in the course, you gradually come to understand its content. You will be learning about the subject from the teacher, the texts, and the other students in the class. What you learn will shape the way you hear the teacher, argue with your classmates, or read the texts.

If we teachers treat you as if you knew nothing about the subject, and if you are afraid to speak for fear of being wrong, then you will become passive. You will wait for us to tell you what you think, and then you will write it down, and tell it back to us in papers and on exams. In this kind of system, there is little reward for thinking on your own. There is also little reward for listening to other, apparently equally ignorant students. This is why students often complain about group work of any kind. They want to know why the teacher does not just give them the answer.

Collaborative learning asks that you

- Have the courage to recognize and speak your own ideas.
- Respect the ideas and knowledge that other students bring to the class.
- Trust the teacher to listen to you with respect and to care about your ideas.

Collaborative learning redefines your relationship to your teacher and to the other students in the class. Rather than assume that your mind is a blank slate, waiting to be written on by the teacher, collaborative learning focuses on the knowledge and experiences that you bring to a classroom. It works by finding out what you know and then allowing the teacher to respond and give you exercises that will let you learn. The teacher does not digest all the knowledge and feed it to you like the predigested food fed to baby birds. The teacher does not report her learning. You learn for yourself, and the teacher is there as a kind of coach to guide your learning, to point you to important ideas and books, to give you exercises that will help you sharpen your skills.

Although the teacher does not direct your learning in a collaborative classroom, collaborative learning is neither free nor unstructured. Instead it is a new structure in which the teacher sets tasks and you complete them in order to discover and explore ideas. This kind of classroom will allow you to explore knowledge as it is constructed by individuals working together to determine what is true. Much of what we "know" is actually agreed-upon knowledge. We make certain assumptions about the physical nature of our world, but those assumptions change each time we make new discoveries about the atom or the galaxy. We say that we "know" what a poem means or how the ancient Romans built roads, but our "knowledge" is always changing as we uncover new evidence, sort through it to determine whether or not we believe it, and reconstruct our world views. In a historical study of writing groups, Anne Ruggles Gere describes how collaborative learning works.

> Participants in collaborative groups learn when they challenge one another with questions, when they use the evidence and information available to them, when they develop relationships among issues, when they evaluate their own thinking. In other words, they learn when they assume that knowledge is something they can help create rather than something to be received whole from someone else.

Collaborative learning does not focus on opinions (personal beliefs), but rather on beliefs accepted by a group as knowledge. Not all observations and interpretations are considered equally valid by the academic community — the group that you join in attending a college or university. In this class, you will participate in the process of making knowledge.

As you will probably see, collaborative learning takes a lot of work on your part. It is not easy for either you or the teacher, since both of you are working in a new way. You have to learn to trust your ideas and to share them, while the teacher has to learn how to stop giving you information and help you discover that information on your own. But I think that you will find the effort worthwhile. Don't be surprised if some of the class takes to collaborative learning more readily than others. Don't assume that students who immediately seem to enjoy working together are the "best" students in the class. Differences in family background, cultural differences, and preferences based on learning styles all affect how well someone likes collaborative learning.

Exercise on Previous Collaborative Learning Experiences. Think about a time when you had to work collaboratively. You may remember a family project like building a garage or a school project like putting on a play. Did you find it easy to work with others? Make a list of what you liked or did not like about this collaborative project.

Now get together with two to four other students (your teacher may assign you to a group) and compare notes. Make a list of all the things that you as a group liked about working together and a list of all the things that you dreaded. The items on your list should not be redundant. It is possible, however, that the same feature of collaboration could appear on both lists. Try to be as specific as possible. If some members of the group liked the energy that a group can generate and others did not, try to explain why some enjoy working in groups and others do not. You might say, for example, that your group likes the excitement that a group generates, but dislikes it when that energy is distracting.

Your teacher will ask the group to read their lists to the entire class. If you look at the list of what people dislike about collaboration, you will know some of the issues that this class may explore.

WRITING TOGETHER

Students communicate with their teachers primarily through writing — papers, lab reports, and exams. So, as you learn to work collaboratively, you will probably need to write together as well. You may edit each other's individual work, or you may actually compose papers together. Therefore, learning how to collaborate when writing is important for students.

More than most people, writers need to work together. Of course, as I sit here at my word processor, I am alone in my study. No one is here working with me. But as I click these keys, I am thinking about all the conversations that I have had with colleagues about writing and about collaboration. Some of these "conversations" were never spoken — they were carried on in letters or through the books in the library. And tomorrow I will print up this chapter and send it to several of my students and friends to see how they like it. They will give me helpful advice. Some may like my ideas; others may not. These people will become ghostly co-authors of this book. I would never think of sending my work to a publisher without first asking several friends to read and comment on it. I need readers.

In my first year of college, however, I did not think of writing as a social activity. Sure, I complained to my friends about having to write this paper or that, and occasionally I asked them about how their papers were going. But when I sat down to write, I can remember vividly facing this image of a blank wall. I stared and stared at that wall, hoping that by concentrating long enough I would suddenly find something to say. Usually I kept staring until the deadline for the paper forced me to write *something*. Most of my papers that year were a thin mixture of plot summary and the ideas I had heard in class. I didn't really think of writing as sharing my thoughts and opinions with someone; instead I saw it as fulfilling an assignment by showing the teacher that I had read the book. It never occurred to me that I could talk with friends about the material that I was reading and that those discussions might give me ideas for a paper. I could only imagine the teacher reading my paper, nodding when she agreed and shaking her head when I was wrong.

Now that I am a writer and a teacher, I look at writing differently. I share my work with my friends and discuss it with my family. I also know that when teachers read papers, they are not just searching for and correcting errors. When teachers read papers, they want to know what students are thinking. Most important, I know that in order to write something, I need to talk to people first. I need to go to a meeting and try my ideas out on people. I need to hear others' ideas and respond to them. I cannot write just by looking at a blank wall and searching my mind. I form ideas by being part of a thinking, talking, writing community.

In Chapters 3 and 4, this book will introduce two different kinds of collaborative writing. Sometimes, you will work with others only when you revise. This situation is very much like that in which most professionals write, whether they are engineers, chemists, storytellers, newspaper reporters, anthropologists, or business people. Most people share ideas with their colleagues, write alone, and then submit their work to their friends and/or their co-workers for comments and revision. Usually this kind of paper is signed by an individual, although other people may be acknowledged for their contributions.

Another kind of collaborative writing is co-authored work. A committee within the Republican party writes a platform describing the party's values and goals. A research group writes a grant proposal. Or a public relations department summarizes its work in an annual report. All of these documents are written by committees because they must represent the ideas held in common by a group of people. Sometimes individuals draft sections of a group report and then the whole group edits it. Other times, a large group plans the content and form of a document, which is then written by one person and edited by another. In either case, this is the kind of document that is signed by many different people, indicating that a group is responsible for the content of the report or proposal.

Exercise on Previous Collaborative Writing Experiences.   Have you ever done any collaborative writing? Have you commented on other students' work, or worked on a group research project? If you have done this kind of writing, make notes about what you enjoyed in the process and what you did not enjoy. If you have never done this kind of writing before, take notes about what you think you will enjoy or not enjoy.

Now get together with two to four other students (your teacher may assign you to a group) and compare notes. Make a list of all the things that you as a group like about collaborative writing and a list of all the things that you dread. The items on your list should not be redundant. It is possible, however, that the same feature of collaborative writing could appear on both the list of likes and the list of dislikes. Try to be as specific as possible. If some group members enjoy sharing ideas and others do not, try to explain why. You might say, for example, that members of your group like hearing about others' good ideas, but dislike having to donate their good ideas to the group and lose individual "credit" for them.

Your teacher will ask the group to read their lists to the entire class. If you look at the list of what people dislike about collaborative writing, you will know some of the problems that this class may explore.

BENEFITS OF COLLABORATIVE LEARNING

If you did the preceding exercises, you probably uncovered some of the drawbacks to collaborative learning. It takes time. Sometimes it is hard for a group to meet together. Some group members may work harder than others. But collaborative learning also has many benefits. You are more likely to remember what you learn collaboratively because you always link new ideas and information to what you already know. In collaborative learning, you will find that you spend a good bit of time putting concepts into your own language or teaching them to others. But, even more important, collaborative learning teaches you how to work together in a group. Schools generally teach you to compete; jobs generally require you to cooperate. The past president of my university received a letter from a biological research firm that had hired two of our graduates. The employer complimented the university president on how well the graduates knew biology. But, he said, when the recent graduates were put in a research pool with other biologists and asked to work together to solve a difficult problem, the scientists competed to see which of them could solve the problem fastest individually. As a result, the problem did not get solved by that group. These research biologists are like most of the people in a recent survey who said that they worked in groups a good deal but had never been trained to do so. Most wished that they had had this training before they had to learn how to work together on the job.

Collaborative learning is especially helpful when you are writing. It is essential to have other people to talk with and to be your readers. When you write alone, it is hard to read your work objectively, to see where you've been clear and where obscure. Because writing involves both a writer and a reader, it almost demands to be investigated collaboratively. Albert Bernstein, a clinical psychologist, describes this difference clearly.

> When I am writing alone, I always visualize an audience, but I hear my own experiences. . . . It's kind of a closed loop—there's no input from anyone else. When I'm working with other people there are several things that I must keep in mind: not just what the audience might say but what the person I'm working with is going to think of this line. . . . Working with someone else gives you another point of view. There is an extra voice inside your head; that can make a lot of difference. Others can see things about what I am doing or what I am saying that I can't see.

As Karen Spear notes in her book *Sharing Writing*, writing skills and interpersonal skills are very similar — learning to anticipate your reader's questions and needs is very much like learning to live productively and harmoniously in a community, whether that community is a family, a town, or a university.

Of course, technology is going to make collaboration even more efficient. Computer networks now allow me to co-author an article with someone in another state by exchanging drafts electronically. Many of you may be writing on word processors, and these machines will help you revise with very little mechanical effort. FAX machines send material around the world in seconds, allowing scientists, artists, and other researchers to share their work more easily.

As you can tell, I think that collaborative learning is really wonderful. I do not mean to imply, however, that all classes should be taught through collaborative learning all the time. People learn differently, and there is a time when lectures are the most efficient way to communicate ideas. If all classes were run collaboratively all the time, students and teachers alike would be frantic for some simple way to convey basic information. We need textbooks, libraries, teachers, laboratories, and each other to learn. Some subjects and skills are also more easily learned alone. Your teacher may well intermingle collaborative and traditional learning activities, and I hope that you will find both methods helpful. You will have to work harder when you learn collaboratively than when you are presented pre-packaged information in easily digested lectures. But I believe that you will also learn more.

Exercise on Methods of Effective Learning and Teaching.   I have just written about how I think that my students learn best. There are, however, many different ways of thinking about learning. Write notes for yourself on the class, teacher, or assignment that has taught you the most. Why did you learn from it? Do not feel that you have to talk about collaborative learning; this exercise should help you learn what you think—not replicate what I think. Try to be as specific as possible. If you want to discuss a class or a teacher, focus on a single day in that class or a class project that was typical of why the course was useful. After about ten minutes of thinking and taking notes, write down three sentences that sum up why or how this class, teacher, or assignment invited you or forced you to learn.

Now get together with two to four other students (your teacher may assign you to a group) and compare your conclusions. What, if anything, was common in your experiences? As a group, write three sentences that reflect the group's experience. In some cases, you may find that you all readily agree—that in fact you've all written a similar set of sentences. In other cases, you may have to look carefully at your conclusions in order to find common denominators. Or, you may find that your group disagrees and that your final statements will include contradictions. If this is the case, try to explain in your final sentences how these conclusions arise from different contexts. Your final sentences might begin something like, "When you are trying to learn a practical process like auto body repair . . ." or "If you've always found school easy . . . ."

Remember that there are no "right" answers to this exercise. The purpose is for you to reflect on your own schooling and compare your thoughts with those of your classmates. After your group has written its conclusions, the teacher will ask each group to report so that you have a sense of how others in the class feel about learning. You may be asked to hand in your individual and group sentences.

Exercise on Defining Collaborative Learning.   In a group of three or four, create analogies for collaborative learning as you now understand it. Is collaborative learning like being coached in a team sport? Or is it like a group of blind men trying to create a camel? Decide on the basic outlines of your group's analogy and sketch out its details in the group. Then, as individuals, write up your sense of the analogy, pointing out where it works and where it does not. The analogy should begin, "Collaborative learning is like . . . ." It will probably take you one or two pages to explain the analogy completely. You may hand these papers in to the teacher, or she may ask you to read your analogies to the class.

Exercise on the Benefits of Working Together and Alone.   Whether you prefer to work mostly with others or by yourself, you will probably acknowledge that each of these procedures can be useful at times. Working by yourself, make two lists defining the kinds of situations when it is better to work together and to work alone. Do not list tasks as specific as, say, repairing a washing machine, but instead list features of repairing a washing machine that make it more appropriate for an individual or a group project. Then, in your group, compare lists and compile a composite list. When necessary, qualify statements so that everyone in the group accepts the final list. Be prepared to read your list to the class or submit it to the teacher.

SUGGESTED PAPER TOPICS

1. Describe your most recent collaborative learning experience. This experience may have taken place in school, at work, or at home. As you relate the experience, try to convey your attitude toward it by the kinds of words that you choose to describe the activity.

2. Define collaborative learning, combining the information supplied in this chapter with your own experience.

3. Compare and contrast working together and working alone in reference to a specific activity like cooking. What makes cooking alone fun? What makes cooking together fun? When would you rather cook alone and why?

4. Interview someone who has a career you'd like to have. Ask him what kinds of work he does in collaboration with his colleagues. What skills has he learned to help him work well with others? What does he find most frustrating about collaboration? Write a "feature" story for your college or town newspaper, describing the person you interviewed, the kind of work he does, and his attitudes toward that work.

5. Describe the class, teacher, or assignment that has taught you the most. Why did you learn from it? What made it special? Try to be as specific as possible, focusing on a single day or a specific project. Make your description as vivid as possible so that the reader sees the experience through your eyes.

CHAPTER
2

WORKING
EFFECTIVELY
IN GROUPS

*A*lthough we are all members of many different groups (families, sports teams, schools, clubs), few of us can work effectively in a group. We know that we should work together with other members of the basketball team or with our siblings, but many of us are not good at this kind of cooperation. As a result, this country is filled with broken and dysfunctional families. Team members have been known to sabotage team efforts in order to gain individual glory. In fact, we seem to have accepted our collective defeat at being effective group members; we've stopped trying to work together. We have learned to survive by simply abandoning a group when it no longer meets our needs. So, we often change jobs, change political parties, change neighborhoods, and leave or ignore all or some of our family members. We no longer feel that we must "work it out," and so we "move on." We can accept this state of affairs, because two of our most powerful cultural myths devalue the ability to cooperate.

The first of these myths concerns the "natural advantages" of competition. From the time we are small, Americans are trained to compete. As children, we vie for attention, we learn to play games in which one person loses and another wins, and we compete to have our school papers appear on teachers' bulletin boards. As a society, America is obsessed with competition. We spend our working hours competing for promotions or salary raises, and our leisure time watching or playing competitive sports or "keeping up with the Joneses" by improving our houses. Just listen to the patter that pervades our media. We are sold the "best" toothpaste to give us the "whitest" teeth; we learn that "more" doctors prescribe Bayer aspirin;

we are proud to be "Employee of the Month," to drive a car that is "#1," or to live in a city that pollsters rank as "most desirable." Comparison of this kind is rooted in competition.

The educational system has played a key role in teaching us the importance of competition. Even though most teachers do not use a strict grade curve that would limit the number of A's, the presence of grades implies that teachers are going to judge students comparatively. Rare is the teacher who assigns all her students the same grade. It is no wonder, then, that students have learned to compete for grades. If you have a good idea, you may not want to share it with other students because then it will be less valuable in raising your own grade. We hear stories all the time of students removing crucial library materials so that other students cannot read them. In a recent poll of college freshmen, only 10 percent reported having ever cooperated with another student on a school-related project.

Closely related to our embrace of competition is our faith in individualism. The myths that define our culture enshrine isolated individuals — Paul Bunyan, Davy Crockett, Wild Bill Hickock, Billy the Kid. Rare are the teams like Lewis and Clark. We praise the individualism of the frontier settlers, when in fact American pioneers valued cooperation and relied heavily on their neighbors for survival. Communities were necessary not only for events like barn-raising, but also to clear the land, establish schools and churches, and allow for some specialization of labor. We idolize the self-sufficient pioneer, but few pioneers were really self-sufficient. All relied on goods brought from the big cities. Can you imagine every pioneer building his own iron smelter? Despite our myths, we are a communal animal. We must work together to survive.

If you have worked collaboratively before, this chapter should make you aware of how you work best with others. But most of you will need to learn how to work together effectively in a group. It will not come "naturally," and so you must not get discouraged. Just remember that everyone is trying to learn to cooperate. You are not the only one who may find group work frustrating at first. Cooperation involves a whole new value system, new techniques for interpersonal communication, and new methods for evaluating ourselves and our work.

FORMING A GROUP

Learning groups have been around for a long time. Benjamin Franklin met with a group of his friends in what he called the Junto to share ideas and essays. Seventeenth-century poets like John Herbert and John Donne met in coffeehouses to read each other's work. Mary Shelley's novel, *Frankenstein*, was created as part of an informal writing group involving her husband and their friends. Within schools, too, students and faculty used to form societies to debate political ideas, improve their writing and speaking skills, and socialize. They assigned themselves topics to explore and carried on their debates as extracurricular activities. These societies disappeared only when fraternities began to take over their social functions and English departments became the focus for discussing literature and teaching writing. Many college and university faculty still meet in seminars to share their research and writing. All professions—from pest controllers to bankers, doctors, and quilters—arrange conferences so that they can meet together and exchange ideas. The learning groups that you form in this class will be part of this long tradition.

In this class, you may be able to form your own groups or the teacher may assign you to work with specific other people. Do not be surprised if you are brought together with people you do not know well and who may be different from you. Most groups operate best when they have heterogeneous memberships. If the people in your group are all quite different, then you will each have special backgrounds, knowledge, and talents to bring to your collective task. Some of you will be better at analyzing readings, others will be good researchers, and still others will be proficient negotiators who can help group members talk together usefully. The more frequently you collaborate, the better you will get to know your special strengths and weaknesses as a group member.

Some groups in this class may consist of only two students, while others will be much larger. Obviously, it is easier to work with a smaller group—there are fewer people who have to meet or to agree. When I work with a small number of my colleagues, I always feel much more of a sense of responsibility toward the group. With a large committee, I can count on someone to "cover" for me if I get too busy to complete my assignment fully. But in a small group, I know exactly what I must do and how important my input is. Later in this chapter, I will discuss special concerns for working in a large group.

Getting Acquainted

Whether your group will work together for only one exercise, for a series of exercises, or for the entire course, the first thing that you will need to do is get acquainted. If you have a small group, of course, you may already know each other. But usually you will need to introduce yourselves briefly: "Hi, I'm Jennifer and I'm from Detroit. I think I'll probably major in engineering." In a large group, you may want to make name tags and prop them on your desks or on the tables in front of you. You will learn names more quickly if you see them all the time associated with faces. When you work with the same group on a long project or series of projects, you will have an opportunity to learn more about your collaborators. Knowing people's backgrounds helps you respond to each other as whole people. It is important that you learn as much as possible about other people in your group so that you can work together and negotiate efficiently over a long period of time. There are several ways to do this. Here are two suggested exercises.

Exercise to Get Acquainted.   Divide into pairs. One of you should interview the other for three minutes, asking about the person's background, interests, habits, and so on. Your teacher will indicate when three minutes have gone by. Then switch roles as interviewer and interviewee. After three minutes have passed, each of you can introduce your new acquaintance to the rest of the group. These presentations should take about one minute each. The presentations might sound something like this:

> This is Gregor. He's from a small town in Wisconsin where his family runs a clothing store. He went to school at Neenah Public High School and spent most of his time there singing in the choir and playing basketball. He hasn't done much math, and so he's a little worried about this class.

Using this method, it should take about 15 minutes for a group of four people to get to know each other fairly well.

Variation: Exercise for Quick Introductions.   If you have less time for introductions, go quickly around the group, giving your name, hometown, and an answer to the question, "If you suddenly received one million dollars, what would you do with it?"

If your group is going to be doing any work outside the class, you will also want to exchange names and phone numbers (or electronic mail addresses if you work on a computer network) so that you can reach each other quickly. You may think that you will never need to find each other outside class, but you may be surprised. What if one of you got sick? Do not count on campus directories or your memory.

THE GROUP PROCESS

After you are acquainted with your group, you will need to complete four simple tasks. If you are working with one or two other people on a clearly defined project, like commenting on each other's papers, this will take only a minute at most. If, however, you are part of a large research team that will collaborate for three or four weeks on a complicated project, this procedure will take more time and effort.

Defining the Problem

As with individual work, it is extremely important that you know what the problem or assignment is before you try to work on it. Have you ever found out after you've written an entire paper that you misunderstood what was being asked? It is well worth taking time to be sure that you know what you want to do before you do it. This kind of understanding is especially important when you work collaboratively, since the whole group needs to be addressing the same problem. If, for example, your assignment is to write a report on some aspect of Zionism, you will want to be sure that everyone agrees about whether this report should be historical, theoretical, persuasive, or whatever. You will also have to agree on your audience and purpose for the report so that when you begin to share ideas, individuals within the group are working toward the same goal. If such basic assumptions are not shared, then the group will not communicate well.

Your assignments for collaborative learning will be quite varied, and so you will want to repeat this process with each one — even if you are working with only one other person. Begin by analyzing the assignment as it was handed to you. You may want to ask questions like:

How is this assignment similar or different from others that we have done?

What terms in the assignment have been featured in recent classes? Do we understand those terms?

If there is a written product, who are we writing to? What should the final product look like?

Comparing the assignment to past assignments, exercises, and class discussion or lectures will help you understand the purpose of the assignment within the course as a whole.

Defining Subtasks and Assigning Individual Responsibility

Once you understand the nature of the task assigned to you, make a list of the various things that must be done in order to complete the project. In some cases, like the following computer science assignment, the list will have only a few items:

Read the problem carefully. What must this computer program do exactly?

Break the program down into subroutines. Assign subroutines to individuals for them to complete.

As a group, integrate subroutines.

Run and debug program.

In other cases, the subtasks may be quite numerous. For example, let's assume that you are working with a group to compile a collection of essays on early black women playwrights. Although each member of the group will write an individual essay, the collection of essays will work together to address a central concern. You need to coordinate your efforts and do lots of planning for a project like this. Here are some steps you might follow.

Do library research to generate a list of playwrights that we might consider. (What is "early" anyway?)

Decide on the playwrights we will discuss.

Read plays written by those playwrights and think about them.

Read secondary material (criticism) on the playwrights and on early black drama.

Meet to share research, determine a central concern for the collection, decide on topics for individual papers, and sketch out our essays.

Meet to read drafts and respond to them.

Revise individual papers.

Meet to write an overview introduction.

As the project proceeds, you will want to modify this list of tasks, in this case probably by determining which plays the entire group will read and have in common. But this list is a place to begin. It gives you a road map so that you all know where you are going.

Once the subtasks are outlined like this, you can begin to assign work to individual group members. Try to be as equitable as possible — everyone should feel equally important and responsible. Therefore, if one task seems less significant than another, make that task only part of an individual's assignment. As you assign jobs, take into account any special talents or backgrounds that your collaborators might have. For example, a group member with a background in American history might be the best person to explore the theatre scene in general. Someone with a background in Afro-American studies might be interested in looking at the state of black drama during this period.

Determining a Timetable

Now you are ready to agree on a timetable for this project. As a team, begin to assign due dates for each stage of the process. Remember to consider how one stage may rely on the work of a preceding stage. For example, how can the group writing on black women playwrights know who they want to write about until their library research is done? In assigning tasks and establishing due dates for them, be sure to consider commitments that individuals may have (work schedules, other course assignments, sports). And check to be sure that no one is given too many things to do simultaneously. Remember that a group can procrastinate just as an individual can — but if all the individuals in the group procrastinate (especially at different times and rates), you will simply get frustrated with each other and never complete your assignment. It is important that everyone agree on the schedule and have a clear copy of it. You can avoid many misunderstandings if everyone is working from the same timetable.

Of course, your calendar is always subject to revision. A more detailed list of steps to be followed would probably include time to reconsider and revise the timetable if necessary. For this reason, I always include a "fudge factor" in my timetables, whether for group or individual work. Someone may get sick. Library materials may not be available. Research may turn up a problem that you hadn't anticipated. The computer could devour your text. Put some breathing space into your schedule so that you can deal with these problems more comfortably.

Providing for Ongoing Evaluation

As you look over your plan of action, consider ways in which the group can monitor itself. In traditional classes, you usually count on the teacher to evaluate your progress and help you modify your plans accordingly. But, in this class, each team should direct itself. Some projects will allow individuals in the group to work fairly independently for most of the project. If you are gathering information and writing separate sections of a report and if your research does not rely on the research done by others in your group, you can probably work alone. In other cases, like the project on black women playwrights, the team will need to meet regularly in order to be sure that everyone is doing their work and to exchange information.

When you do meet to assess your progress on a particular project, try to be as honest as possible. Don't lie to your group and tell them that everything is "OK" if it's not. In this society, we are trained to hide our problems —unless we are talking to a psychiatrist or a talk show host. When someone asks, "How are you?" few people respond truthfully. We just say, "OK. How are you?" Don't let this kind of formulaic response creep into your group's self-evaluation. Plan to monitor your own progress several times as you work on the assignment, so no more than a week passes without some kind of reality check. Usually, this means that the group will need to meet outside of class.

BEING AN EFFECTIVE GROUP MEMBER

Communicating Your Thoughts

Communicating your thoughts may seem like quite a natural process, but it is a skill that we all need to work on. When speaking in your group, remember to make your language as specific and accurate as possible. Instead of saying, "That's a bad idea," say something like "If we do that, it will take a lot of work." Be sure to avoid jargon or vague terms that may not be understood in the same way by all the group members. I sometimes have trouble communicating with my students if they use personal or generational jargon. I remember my sister-in-law telling me that my wardrobe was "preppy." I didn't know what she meant, and I wasn't at all sure whether she was envying me or telling me to throw my clothes away. It took a long time for me to understand this term, and now I use it frequently. I've lost my sensitivity to the fact that everyone else won't necessarily understand the word.

In addition to avoiding personal or technical jargon, you need to be aware of other vague terms that we use frequently when we speak. Some of these vague words are heavily charged with emotion. When some speakers say "liberal," for example, they mean "open-minded and unselfish," while others mean "hopelessly idealistic" or "recklessly iconoclastic." Listen to see if you rely heavily on words like "important" (if something is important, say how and why), "significant" (what makes it significant?), "democratic" (in what sense?), and "stupid" (how?). If I tell you that an article I read was "phenomenal," you won't know much about the article except that I liked it. If, however, I tell you that the article was "thorough, insightful, and entertaining," you may be better prepared to decide if you want to read it, too.

You will also strengthen group communication if you avoid ambiguity. If you have an opinion, say so. Don't attribute that opinion to "many people" or to an anonymous "they." Also work to match your body language to your words. It is hard to know what someone means when she says, "That's a good idea," and frowns. Finally, be sure that you call people by name rather than referring to them as "he" or "she" or even "you." If you say, "Let's do what he suggests," others may not understand which "he" you are referring to. In traditional classrooms, teachers often preserve students' anonymity. We look at a sample student paper, but we don't know who wrote it. This kind of anonymity just won't work in a collaborative setting. If you have an idea, *own* it. If someone else had a good idea, use their name when you talk about the idea. If you can't remember who said something, then say that: "I don't remember who suggested this, but I think it was a good idea."

This is not to imply that all your remarks need to be lengthy. Try to speak as concisely as possible, but without sacrificing clarity or completeness. Explain your idea or reaction and the reason you feel that way, and then stop talking. You will have to do a lot of work in a short amount of time in these groups, and no one wants to listen endlessly to one person. Finally, it is important that you look directly at the people you are talking to and ask them if they understand what you're saying. Watch people's faces for signals that you are communicating clearly or not.

Trusting and Valuing Your Own Knowledge

In the first chapter, I said that when I was a student, I learned that it was better to be quiet than to be wrong. I hope that you will never have to feel that way. I hope that you already value what you know and think, so that you can contribute to a discussion fearlessly. Ideas grow only when they can be put into language, and there's nothing better to stimulate their growth than exchanging ideas with others. Although I used to be afraid to speak in class, now I collaborate in all aspects of my life. I cannot imagine trying to think through a problem without talking to others. I have learned to value what I can bring to a group project and to trust my voice in conveying it. This section offers you some suggestions that may help you to speak honestly in a group.

When I am working with a group, I must work hard to remember that people are not always judging me and that they are just as uncertain as I am. If I think of the people around me as smarter and more articulate, I cannot speak. But if I think of them as no smarter than I am, I can voice my ideas. A large part of what society calls "shyness" is rooted in a fear of being thought stupid, wrong, old-fashioned, or whatever.

One sure way to feel that you can speak in a group is to be prepared. If you have done your work, you will have authority to speak. Before the group meets, you might review for yourself what you have to say ("My research confirms what Marissa said") and what is worrying you and needs to be discussed ("What do we do if this library book cannot be found?"). You may even want to write down notes to yourself, a kind of private agenda for the meeting. During a meeting, I always keep notes about things I want to say. That way, if an idea comes to me but I cannot break into the conversation at that point, I will remember the idea later. These notes also help me keep track of my own thoughts as the conversation swirls around me. I sometimes take two columns of notes, one recording what others say or what the group decides, and the other showing my reactions or questions.

I have been stressing the importance of recognizing that you have something to contribute to the group. But you must also realize that your ideas may not always be adopted. If you have a strong feeling, don't back off from it immediately. Sometimes you can convince the group that you're right. But don't insist on having things your way all the time. You must value your own point of view, but you must also recognize others' points of view.

The Fine Art of Listening

Just as important as good speaking skills are good listening skills. We often think of listening as a reflex that is activated automatically when sound reaches the ear. But there is a difference between merely hearing a sound and actually listening to it. Have you ever asked a question only to discover that the same question was asked and answered minutes earlier? The first step in good listening is attentiveness. Far from being passive, listening requires steady concentration.

But listening is more than hearing and comprehending what a speaker is saying. Listening involves attending so closely to speech that you understand the speaker's message, meaning, motive, and tone. Sometimes you will find that people say one thing and mean something quite different. You must learn to listen as carefully as you read — attending to both the immediate message (what's being said) and underlying meanings. The best listeners can point out when two people agree, even though they seem to disagree, and vice versa. Look at the following conversation, for example.

> SUNG: *Huckleberry Finn* is racist. Just look at how Huck treats Jim — they're never really equals. Well, maybe when they're on the raft. But when they're ashore, Huck treats Jim like he would any other slave, and Twain doesn't criticize him for it.

> MARIA: C'mon, Twain wasn't a racist. Look at how similar Huck and Jim are. Black, white — it makes no difference to Twain. And see how kind Huck is when he's on the raft? Whenever he can be kind to Jim, he is.

It is clear in this exchange that Sung and Maria are defining "racist" quite differently. Sung defines a racist as someone who treats members of another race poorly in public, while Maria defines a racist as one who always treats other races badly. Sung measures a character by his worst behavior and Maria judges one by his best behavior. Maria and Sung agree that Huck treats Jim differently on the raft than on shore, but they judge these actions by applying different criteria. These two people could begin to understand one another's positions by exploring these similarities and differences.

One way to be sure that you understand what someone is saying is to tell him what you heard. I often find myself saying, "Do you mean . . . ?" or "Now, what you seem to be saying is. . . . Is that right?" Be sure that you understand what you're being told before you respond. Lots of arguments escalate when people jump to conclusions and argue without listening carefully to one another.

In addition to listening to what someone says, try to be sensitive to the speaker's motives and tone. If someone seems to defend his position too doggedly, ask yourself why he might feel so defensive. Is his tone a clue to his feelings? Sometimes understanding *why* a speaker has a particular point of view can be an important clue to understanding him and communicating more effectively with him.

Mary Belenky, Blythe Clinchy, Nancy Goldberger, and Jill Tarule outline two different types of thinking and interacting that people in your group may use. They call these two approaches "separated" and "connected" knowing. Be aware of these differences so that you can respond appropriately.

A. Separate knowers bring to their group propositions that they have developed as fully as possible and that they hope to sell in the free marketplace of ideas. Members must know the rules, but they need not know each other. . . . Separate knowers try to subtract the personality of the perceiver from the perception, because they see personality as slanting the perception or adding "noise" that must be filtered out.

B. In connected-knowing groups, people utter half-baked half-truths and ask others to nurture them. Since no one would entrust one's fragile infant to a stranger, members of the group must learn to know and trust each other. In such an atmosphere members do engage in criticism, but the criticism is "connected." . . . Connected knowers see personality as adding to the perception, and so the personality of each member of the group enriches the group's understanding. Each individual must stretch her own vision in order to share another's vision. Through mutual stretching and sharing the group achieves a vision richer than any individual could achieve alone.

As you can see, my advice has been largely that you combine these perspectives as much as possible. If you find this balancing act impossible, however, I believe that you will be a more effective group member if you practice connected knowing by trying to understand others and stretching to share their vision.

NEGOTIATING DIFFERENCES

Perhaps the hardest work any group undertakes is to negotiate differences among its members. Here you are, all working as hard as possible to fulfill an assignment, and you can't agree. What do you do? The first step is to realize that controversy is good. Without different perspectives, the world would be a pretty dull place. But controversy does not necessarily mean aggressive debate. Think of your group's interaction as a conversation. No one's point of view should be ignored. The goal is not necessarily to agree, but rather to understand each other and to let your ideas grow and evolve together.

When you work with other people, you are usually trying to reach a consensus. That does not mean that every member of the group must conform, or that the minority finally gets "voted down." Rather, it means uncovering points of agreement, delineating points of disagreement, and trying to reach a solution that is acceptable to everyone. Norman Holland, a literary critic, says that the original meaning of "consensus" was "feeling or sensing together . . . a crossing of the barrier between ego and ego." In a group trying to reach consensus, you are not working to persuade others, to sell them your idea. You are trying to understand one another and let your ideas enrich each other. You will struggle together to make sense of what you all know. This process should be very familiar. All Americans have the chance to debate the strengths of various presidential candidates, and each registered voter has an opportunity to voice an opinion. But even those people supporting the losing candidate must find a way to work with the winner. The differences of opinion do not disappear, yet the many sides must reach consensus about laws, budgets, and foreign policy, or the nation would cease to function. During the process of reaching consensus, ideas will grow and change; they will not simply be proposed and voted in or out. This is why the communication skills discussed earlier in this chapter are so important.

Consensus is important in the classroom because in the process of moving toward consensus, the various factions within a group will come to understand one another's positions better. If you only talk with people who agree with you, you never learn very much about what you think. Anyone who disagrees with you seems wrong from the start. An environmentalist and an industrialist may never reach full agreement, but it is important for them to talk. They must establish some kind of relationship so that they can work in the same state. So, too, it is fine if your classroom group cannot reach total agreement. That is not necessarily the goal. But remember that sometimes even the most apparently outrageous ideas turn out to be worth considering. Think of how strange many innovators and geniuses — Galileo, Newton, Gandhi, Andy Warhol, Susan B. Anthony — may have seemed to their contemporaries. The efforts to reach consensus are valuable exchanges of opinion that may or may not produce agreement within the group.

Negotiating disputes is a valuable skill in all parts of your life. You will use it in personal relationships, on the job, and in the classroom. The most important thing to remember when you are trying to resolve differences with someone is that the two of you are wrestling with a common problem. Rather than thinking of the situation as a competition in which one side will win and the other lose, remember that both sides can have valid arguments. Begin by uncovering any areas in which the two or more differing sides agree. At some level, you will probably find agreement. The most outspoken right-to-life advocate and the staunchest pro-choice supporter, for example, will probably agree on some ideas like the value of life and the need for guidelines to help young and confused mothers.

Having explored areas of agreement, begin to explore points of disagreement. Are the disagreements factual? Philosophical? Personal? The ongoing debate over abortion, for example, usually finds opponents differing in their definitions of "life." Some look at life from a biological standpoint, others from a religious point of view, and still others from a personal perspective. If the various sides of this debate come to understand one another, then even if they can never agree, they may stop pointless name-calling. Your group can follow a similar procedure. Find out why you differ about whether Hamlet is sane or Freud was sexist. In discovering areas of agreement and disagreement, you will learn.

Talking to someone who disagrees with you can be difficult. Be sure that you understand what she is saying. Paraphrase her point of view accurately and non-evaluatively. Instead of saying, "Your argument is full of holes — it's obviously wrong," you will want to say, "So, you believe that Hamlet is insane because no sane man would see ghosts and talk to them." Then present your own point of view with equal precision: "Well, I disagree because I've met ghosts and talked with them, but I think that I'm sane." There will be times when you want to include the speaker's feelings in your paraphrase of his point of view. You may want to say, "You seem to think that Hamlet's murder of his stepfather is wrong, and you blame him by calling him insane."

Be careful when paraphrasing, however, that you avoid judgment, and that you respond to ideas, not to people. Don't say, "Well, where you come from, I guess murder is commonplace and so you approve of it, but I have morals!" Remember that every member of the group wants to feel free to talk without being belittled. If the group members begin to put each other down, then soon no one will want to contribute to the debate. You can be supportive of one another by remaining open and listening, without having to accept ideas uncritically. At some point in the discussion, it may be useful for opposing sides to try to assume each other's perspectives. If you believed what your opponents believe, what would you say? This kind of role-playing is an excellent exercise for developing a position paper, and it can foster understanding.

When you are trying to understand someone else's beliefs, look for the key terms in that argument. Are they defined so that you can both agree about them? In the conversation between Sung and Maria (p. 22), we saw how those two people were talking about a key idea—racism—and yet were using the word to mean different things. You will also want to see if both sides are making the same kinds of arguments. If a woman from Chicago is convicted of spying, one person might say she is not an American, and another disagree. From a legal standpoint, she is still a citizen unless the courts take that citizenship away as part of her punishment. But, from a moral standpoint, she is not acting like a good citizen. In order to understand this dispute, you need to see that the two perspectives—legal and moral—are at odds. Let me provide one more example. Suppose a man is arguing with his son about values. The man thinks values are very important and he is quite upset that his son's values are different. Now, he could reject his son's values as wrong. Or he could reason that values are always changing, and so his values and his son's are inevitably different since they arise from different times and environments. He may still disapprove of his son's beliefs, but he can now understand why his son is different. He may even come to see how his son has adopted and adapted some of his own beliefs.

When a collaborative group meets, it is not to debate final positions but rather to converse and construct new ideas and interpretations. Many collaborative exercises will ask you to form an individual opinion before you meet as a group. This does not mean that the group then "votes" on the best ideas brought to it, or that everyone's contributions are "judged." If the members of your group seem to hold contests to see whose idea is best, raise this issue. Yes, the group will sometimes have to reject certain ideas and emphasize others. This is quite natural. But the goal of the group is to include responses, to enrich the group's understanding through the multiple perspectives of its members.

As the group makes decisions about how it will present its consensus, make sure that everyone shares responsibility for the final group position.

Do not make decisions without notifying the entire group. If you should determine, for example, that a minority view is not relevant or not different enough to warrant separate presentation, be sure that you decide this as a group. How would you feel if your minority position were suddenly excluded from a final report? I want to make clear that I am advocating understanding, not necessarily agreement. Do not be afraid to change your mind if and when you feel that you are wrong. Pigheadedness is not a virtue. But do not be falsely accommodating. The world would be a dangerous place if people did not try to understand each other, but it would also be incredibly boring if we always agreed.

Exercise on Recognizing Bias.   Look at the following paragraph. As individuals, paraphrase the main idea in a phrase or sentence. Circle words that are loaded and indicate the writer's feelings about his topic. Then, in your group, compare notes and revise the paragraph so that it either shows as little bias as possible or flows from an opposite set of values. (Your teacher will tell you which of these options he would like you to follow.)

> Tricked at every turn by Communists and other white people, the Invisible Man falls prey to his own people's instinct toward violence and subversion. He almost kills a white man just for calling him names — using his natural physical superiority to bully the white man; instead of getting a job, he listens to jazz records all day in a basement burning bright with electricity he has managed to steal from Monopolated Light and Power. The saddest aspect of the story, I think, is that this promising young black gives up the chance to be educated as a responsible citizen, and chooses the criminal path. He does not recognize the wisdom of Booker T. Washington, a black like him, who urged the race to "cast down your bucket where you are."

Exercise on Analyzing Assumptions.   Working with a small group of three to five others, analyze the kind of assumptions made by a national news show host and his or her guests. First decide which news show you will analyze. At the time that this book is being written, you might consider: "The MacNeil/Lehrer Report" (the second half), "20/20," "Meet the Press," or some segments of a talk show like "Donahue." If you choose a more popular show like "Oprah Winfrey," be sure that the topic for the day has some intellectual content. Analyzing a show in which the audience asks "fan" questions of a star will not be as useful or interesting as analyzing one that discusses legal or ethical issues.

Having decided on the show, the group members should watch it, taking notes about what each speaker says. Pay special attention to the unstated assumptions underlying their explicit statements. Use commercial breaks to reflect on the debate and try to see what assumptions each side is making. If you can audiotape or videotape the show, do so.

Then, as a group, compare your notes. Do you agree about the explicit positions that each side takes? Do you agree about the assumptions? Can you see where the lines of the debate are drawn? What is really at stake? Prepare a written or oral report to the class (your teacher will tell you which she wants), briefly summarizing the debate and examining the assumptions that underlie the different positions. Be as specific as possible. If you can quote the speakers, do so.

This exercise can be especially interesting if different groups within the class watch the same show on different nights. Then, after the reports by each group, the class as a whole can see if they can agree about consistent assumptions that the host holds.

Exercise on Assumptions and Audiences.   We are surrounded by advertisements, and this exercise will give you a chance to "fight back." Individually, pick a TV, radio, or print advertisement that you find particularly offensive or troubling. (If you choose a TV or radio ad, write out a transcription of it.) Examine its language and assumptions carefully. How does the ad define its audience? What does it assume about their values and needs? Revise the advertisement, giving the same sales pitch, but making the ad's hidden assumptions obvious.

For example, instead of the pervasive romantic ads telling us that "Diamonds are forever," you might write an ad that says something like, "Do you want to get married and have it last forever? Do you think that anything long-lasting must be good? Do you think that you can live in a fairy tale where people live 'happily ever after'? Then buy a diamond because diamonds last forever."

When you have written your advertisements, share them with your group and talk about how you uncovered the ad's hidden assumptions. Now collaborate with your group to write a simple pamphlet called "Don't be Fooled: How to Read Advertisements." Assume that the pamphlet will be distributed at large supermarkets across the country. When all the groups in the class have completed their pamphlets, you will want to share them and see how they are alike and different. How did various groups try to get the audience to read the pamphlet? How did your advice differ? Why?

PROTECTING AND SHARING IDEAS IN WRITING

This is the hardest dynamic for most of us to understand. We know intuitively that everything we think was probably shaped in some way by something someone else thought or said or wrote. We try to make sense of our relationships with our lovers or our family by thinking of them in the context of all such relationships that we have heard about through friends, television, and books. Even when we sit alone in a quiet room and think by ourselves, our heads are filled with others' voices. This is important to remember when you start to collaborate. But the act of writing has come to be associated with a claim to ownership. And so when you write together —either relying on others' research or creating a co-authored paper — you will need to know how to distinguish copying from building on someone else's ideas.

We have copyright laws that prevent writers from "stealing" material from other writers. Before the institution of these laws, writers borrowed plots from each other openly. One branch of Shakespeare studies concentrates on his "sources," that is, on identifying the texts that he used as the basis for his plays. The world of real writers is slowly beginning to acknowledge the value of sharing ideas during the writing process. But there are still lawsuits concerning plagiarism, and scholars still argue over how to define when a text has a single author.

Writing in school is subject to even more rigorous "copyright" laws than published writing. Your school may have an honor code that you must append to all your work, stating that you are the "sole author" and received no assistance in writing your essays. Because schools combine the functions of teaching and assessing individual work, student writers have been taught to write in artificial isolation. All sharing has been deemed plagiarism. But no paper is written in isolation. When you write, you must consult books in the library and consider class discussions. You know that when you use printed sources, you need to provide a footnote to those sources. Although footnoting is a complicated matter, it is much simpler than knowing how and when to acknowledge ideas that you get from conversation with others. What is the difference between stealing an idea (plagiarizing it) and building on an idea? How do we share thoughts and still treasure them as "our own"?

Copying versus Building on Ideas

There is a difference between presenting someone else's idea as your own and building on or reacting to that idea. You may think that a single-authored text, like a student's individual paper, does not raise issues of sharing and protecting ideas. But even if an individual voice dominates a discussion or a text, the text may have ghostly co-authors. You may be writing a paper and ask someone to read it and respond. Your essay will probably change as a result of ideas that person gives you, but you will still be the author. This is the situation with most books that list a single author on the title page. Just look at the acknowledgments in the front of these books. Authors need to thank their friends and colleagues who helped them develop their ideas, and they need to express their gratitude to their editors and their family. No one writes alone, even if only one person is named as the author.

If you are talking with a friend and that friend "gives" you a really wonderful idea, can you use it in your paper? There are many answers to this dilemma. Some teachers would say that you cannot use this idea at all, but I think that this kind of restriction can only manacle minds. We all work from other people's good ideas. Other teachers would advise you to use the idea and acknowledge it in some way—in a footnote, within the text ("Chris mentioned that . . ."), or in a prefatory statement modeled after the acknowledgments in a book. I find it most natural when this kind of informal acknowledgment comes as part of the text: "Shari said that the library's labor practices were demeaning. She argued that . . . , but I say. . . ." Here students' ideas are presented in the same form as published ideas. Instead of saying, "Virginia Woolf said," you simply say, "My sister Jo says. . . ."

All these methods are familiar and valid. If, however, you use someone else's idea as a *starting point* for your paper and then react to it or build on it, you may not need to acknowledge it formally. At the early stages of brainstorming, ideas are so raw and unconnected that sharing ideas rarely leads to the same product. If you get an idea from someone else, develop it and make it your own. When you use an idea as a springboard, not as one of the main planks of your paper, you do not need explicit, specific acknowledgment. If, however, you begin and end your essays with an idea that you got from conversation with a friend, then all you have done is supply supporting evidence for her argument. In that case, you are more of a co-author, and I would recommend some form of acknowledgment. It is becoming increasingly common now to see ideas acknowledged in footnotes like: "I would like to thank Dwayne Johnson for first suggesting to me that women's rights and gay rights have different political goals." Beginning a paper or a part of a paper with someone else's idea and building on it is not plagiarism. Importing someone else's idea wholesale and not building on it may be considered plagiarism. This is an important topic to discuss with your friends and your teacher.

So many of our thoughts and feelings are shaped by the people around us that if we were to trace the source of each of our ideas, our papers would be littered with so many attributions that it would be hard to follow them. So, decide whether to acknowledge an idea by the function of that point in your paper. Here is how two students described their interactions with peer readers.

When Tom and I talked about "The Code," I did not particularly agree with everything he said, but we really helped each other in understanding the individual lines. Even when we disagreed on the meaning of a passage, hearing someone else's point of view helped me form my own opinion.

Throughout this experience, whether I was performing or a member of the audience, I think the key was that I was testing my ideas against those of my fellow students. Sometimes it is too easy to accept the opinions of your professor because of their experience and imposing demeanor, but with other students you feel that you are on equal ground. By this interaction, I was forced to scrutinize my own conclusions and rethink many of my first impressions.

These students seem to be developing, not soaking up and spitting out their classmates' ideas. The first one says that he formed his own opinion about the poem even while he was working with other students to clarify it. In other words, he used the conversation about this poem to serve his own ends; the conversation did not define his paper. The other student says that he "tested" his ideas against those of his peers. You can see in this writer's language that the context of peer response has enriched his ideas and may even have altered them, but it has not defined them. Of course, if you are in doubt, acknowledging the work of others is quick and easy to do. It is better to acknowledge their work than to be accused of plagiarism. The distinctions that I am making here may also change slightly from class to class, so if you are in doubt, ask your teacher's advice.

Protecting and Sharing Your Ideas as a Co-Author

When you co-author a text with someone else, the question of who owns what thoughts and phrases is quite different from when you are the sole author. People who collaborate frequently when they write redefine the idea of ownership. Listen to these two statements by people who have written and published books together.

A. In collaborating on writing this book we searched for a single voice — a way of submerging our individual perspectives for the sake of the collective "we." Not that we denied our individual convictions or squelched our objections to one another's points of view — we argued, tried to persuade, even cried at times when we reached an impasse of understanding — but we learned to listen to each other, to build on each other's insights, and eventually to arrive at a way of communicating as a collective what we believe. Hence, this book is not separated into parts that we wish to attribute to one or the other of us, even though each of us took the primary responsibility for different parts. There may be stylistic differences from one section to the next, but the book as a whole is the product of our joint efforts and interchange of ideas. (Mary Belenky, Blythe Clinchy, Nancy Goldberger, and Jill Tarule, *Women's Ways of Knowing.*)

B. We wrote together as an extension and an enrichment of our long friendship. In the process of making each of us present to the other, of hearing our "selves" echoed back and forth, of constituting and reconstituting, forming, transforming, and reforming voices to speak our texts, we came ineluctably to hear within ourselves a large polyphonic chorus rather than just a duet. (Andrea Lunsford and Lisa Ede, *Singular Texts, Plural Authors.*)

These writers are describing what happened as they melded their individual voices into one group voice. In a co-authored book or essay, usually the reader cannot distinguish one person's contribution from another's. The group as a whole is responsible for the text. Some writers experience this formation of one voice as an extension of their own. Albert Bernstein, a clinical psychologist, put it this way: "When I work with other people, one or two other people, I feel that I do a much better job than I would have done alone. I extend myself further and I think I have a clearer idea of what we are trying to do. It brings out more of me so I think it is more mine."

    Problems arise only when an individual feels that she has borne most of the burden of the book. I remember working on a book with four other people. It took us longer to finish the work than we anticipated, and two of the contributors had to leave the project before it was completed. Their work was edited and the final manuscript prepared by only three of the five of us. There was great resentment about this, and, late at night, we would fantasize about leaving the names of the two "deserters" off the book entirely. In the sober light of morning, of course, we realized how much those two had worked, even if they were not with us now. We forgave them and proceeded. If you are co-authoring a paper and feel either exploited or underappreciated, be sure that you talk to your collaborators. Maybe the group does not realize what you have been doing. You are contributing your labor to this project — be sure that it is recognized. But also remember that no one person should dominate a group. The group may have a leader, but it should not produce only the leader's ideas. As an educational researcher told Ede and Lunsford, "Good collaboration rests on a very tenuous relationship. In any kind of group work, there's got to be a lot of give-and-take, and sometimes a lot of giving. And here's the rub: it should have nothing to do with egos."

    In some co-authoring situations, the group brainstorms about the shape of a grant proposal or a business report, and then individuals write separate, identifiable sections. The group as a whole then revises the work. In this situation, you must remember that your name will be identified not only with the entire project but also with your individual statement. As the group edits your statement, you must be sure that you still feel accountable for it. After all, you may be asked to defend it.

Exercise on Using Others' Ideas.   Here is part of a transcript of some students talking about an upcoming paper, along with one student's final work. Did the student plagiarize? If you think that he did not, revise his paper so that it would be plagiarized. If you think that he did plagiarize, then revise the paper to avoid plagiarism, but still retain the basic ideas. Would it make any difference if Owen or Jenn (rather than Leo) were the author of the paper? Discuss this in your group and try to reach a consensus.

The assignment for the paper was

> *Arthur Koestler claims that aliens in science fiction can be "too alien to be true." In that case, he says, "without an act of identification, of intimate understanding, there is no art, only a thrill of curiosity which soon yields to boredom." Agree or disagree with this statement.*

LEO: I don't know what I'm going to write for this paper tomorrow. I really hate this, don't you?

JENN: Yeah, I don't like *any* required course. Um. I'm going to write about um Star Trek.

OWEN: Great! Me, too.

LEO: What show?

JENN: Like the show with the Tribbles. I've seen that rerun about a billion times, you know? I love it when they come crashing through the ceiling.

LEO: Yeah, but did you *identify* with the Tribbles?

OWEN: How could you? They're just dumb dust balls. I mean, they didn't talk or anything. They remind me of my sister's stuffed toys.

LEO: They remind me of baby bunnies — only no ears.

JENN: Well, I liked them. I didn't identify with them, but I understood them. They like just wanted to go on. They wanted to go on living and um growing. I didn't identify with them — well, they weren't like me.

OWEN: You don't want to go on living?

JENN: No, I mean I know they wanted to live, but that's not important. I didn't feel that they were human. But you can be curious about something and like it even if it's not human. That quote's full of it.

LEO: Do you think we're supposed to say that? He's — um — in our book and all. Isn't he supposed to be right?

OWEN: Yea, I think so. Like, the Horta. It was just a rock and all, but it was human. You had to like it or the show didn't make sense. I mean if it was just a rock, why not blast it?

LEO: I don't think that's a good example. How can you — um —

connect with something that's a rock. I could care less about that rock.

JENN: Me too. The Horta and the Tribbles are really different.

LEO: But I really like the bizarre aliens on Star Trek — and the weirder the better. I like seeing just how weird they can get.

OWEN: So, you think the quote's wrong, too.

LEO: No — um — that's not what I said. I don't know. I love Star Trek — I watch it all the time. And, like, I like the aliens, but it's the human story that I care about. I'm curious about the aliens, but I like the people.

JENN: Yeah, I love Captain Kirk — especially when he falls in love with an alien. Sexy. When he fights and gets sweaty —

OWEN: The only Star Treks I don't like are the ones with the giant lizards. Did you see the one where Kirk fights his double in a sort of cloud?

LEO: I like Spock even better than Kirk. What a cool guy. He's really funny, you know?

Here is the paper that Leo wrote after this conversation.

The critic Arthur Koestler has stated that aliens in science fiction are ''too alien to be true'' and that each alien should be given what our instructor has called a ''human reference point.'' I disagree. If the writer is adept at presenting the story in a logical, scientific, and yet enjoyable manner, then I believe that the reader will be open minded enough to accept any form of alien life. One of the most popular episodes of the Star Trek television series featured the Medusan--a mass of twinkling lights that formed images too horrible for the human eye to behold. The Medusan, even with no human features whatever, was believable because of the overall plausibility of the story. The Medusan's highly unusual (to say the least) appearance and repulsiveness to humans was exploited by the writers in such a way that the unlikeliness of its existence was forgotten.

Another example of bizarre alien life, again from Star Trek, is the Horta. Many scientists believe that the only possible form of life is carbon based, as with plants and animals on earth. However, the writers and ''creators'' of the Horta formulated the theory of silicon-based life. Impossible? Perhaps, but the Horta was presented and explained in a manner which made human standards of life unimportant. What <u>was</u> important was the fact that the lives of the Enterprise crew were

endangered. The viewer was involved in a good story and
was more than willing to accept the existence of a very
alien alien.

If one is to agree with Koestler and demand ''human
reference points'' for all science fiction aliens, then
part of the challenge for the author and excitement for
the reader would be lost. Human reference points aren't
important; an imaginative story that is ''true'' for the
human characters is.

SPECIAL CONSIDERATIONS
FOR WORKING WITH A LARGE GROUP

In a bigger group, concerns like finding meeting times, negotiating differences, and balancing workloads loom larger. Unless there are only two of
you in the group, you will want to begin by deciding who will guide the
group and who will keep a record of discussions and decisions so that the
group can report accurately to each other or to the class as a whole. These
positions are like the president or chair and the secretary of a club or
political body. If the group works together for a long time, you will want to
be sure that everyone in the group has a chance to assume each of these
roles at least once. Even though some people may enjoy leading the group
more than others, it is valuable for everyone to try being a leader. After all,
anyone can learn to be a leader and learning to do something can make it
pleasurable.

The Leader's Job

Think of your group leader as a kind of team captain. She guides the team,
assigns special duties, and keeps up morale so that the team as a whole can
do better. The leader is the group's guide, but she does not benefit any
more than any other group member when the group succeeds. The group
works for the equal benefit of each member; it does not "work for" the
leader.

The leader has several important functions. Most important, she keeps
the group focused on the problem at hand. Have you ever tried to plan
something or decide something with a group that kept getting off track? It's
really frustrating — especially if you have limited time. A good leader keeps
the group on track by

- Leading discussion to be sure that the group understands the
assignment.
- Monitoring and guiding discussion to prevent useless digressions.

- Pacing the group's work so that it is completed within the allotted time.

In monitoring and guiding the group's discussion, the leader should encourage as many group members as possible to join in the discussion. If one person is sitting quietly, just watching the group work, the leader needs to ask his opinion. Sometimes just making eye contact with someone will be enough to invite him to speak. The leader should also try to prevent any single person from monopolizing the discussion. If someone wants to talk all the time, the group leader should direct the conversation away from that person. One cardinal rule of all group interaction is *don't interrupt*. If someone interrupts a lot, simply ask that each person be given a chance to speak. I know that it is difficult to ask people to speak or be silent, but sometimes discussing group dynamics can save lots of wasted time later on.

In addition to monitoring the group's discussion, the leader needs to be sure that the group develops a workable procedure for completing the assignment. Of course, the leader should not simply impose a procedure on the group. Instead, she must direct the group to develop a mutually acceptable plan of action. Can the assignment be broken down into parts? And, if so, will the whole group work through each part in sequence, or will individuals or pairs of students attack different parts of the question? Who will do each task? The leader does not answer these questions, but she must be sure that they are asked and answered.

Perhaps the hardest task for the leader is to keep an eye on the clock and pace the group's work. Of course, some groups will always work faster than others, but faster is not necessarily better. Some groups will want to deal with questions so quickly that their answers will be superficial. Leaders of such groups will want to slow down their discussions in order to encourage more depth. On the other hand, slower groups that ponder each part of the question with excessive care may need to work faster toward even a tentative answer so that they can keep up with the class schedule as a whole. Leaders of these groups can nudge them forward by saying things like "This discussion is fascinating, but I remind you that we have to answer three more questions in the next 15 minutes. Does what you're talking about now relate to the next question we need to discuss?"

In addition to watching the group's pace, the leader will want to be sure that the tone of the group's discussion is primarily supportive. There is a difference, as I will say repeatedly, between being supportive and being uncritical. A supportive leader encourages everyone to participate and avoids "put downs" — even those delivered in jest. She need not, however, say "That's a good idea" every time someone speaks.

As you can see, the leader needs to distance herself a bit from the group in order to observe its purpose, direction, pace, and tone. But the leader is also a regular participant in the group. If the leader distances herself too much, she can become like a dictator rather than a group member. If, however, she becomes too involved with the group's conversation and allows the group too much freedom, she will not fulfill her role as leader.

The Recorder's Job

The recorder must also distance himself a bit from the group, without forfeiting his status as a group member. The recorder's job is very important because his notes about the group's discussion will allow them to reconsider ideas, reflect on their methods, or report accurately and completely to the class as a whole. The recorder also keeps a record of any decisions made by the group. For this reason, his voice is most likely to be heard at the beginning of a meeting when he can restate the meeting's goals and at the end of the meeting when he can summarize the discussion and remind the group of its decisions. In summarizing discussion, the recorder will help the group decide what dissent (if any) needs to go "on record" for further investigation or as part of a final report.

The recorder's main concerns are accuracy and completeness. To be accurate, he should report visible behavior and not assume that he understands a speaker's feelings. Therefore, he should write, "Chris pounded the desk and repeated her point" instead of "Chris was adamant and angry." Of course, no one can report an event completely objectively; our own feelings always color our perceptions. So, it is sometimes valuable to know how the recorder felt as he described the group's work. But when the recorder includes his own feelings in his notes, he should label them as such. A recorder should write, "It seemed to me that the group worked real well on this problem" instead of declaring his own reactions as fact: "The group worked well together on this problem." To accomplish this, many recorders take notes on a divided page with the left side for observations and the right side for personal reactions or questions.

As much as possible, the recorder should note the group's behaviors rather than an individual's actions. It is more helpful for the group to know that they decided to divide up a research project into several different subtasks than it is to know that Mike offered a solution, Susan questioned it, and finally Robin supported Mike, and we all agreed with her.

The recorder is also the official publisher for the group. He gets everyone's name and phone number and makes contact sheets for the group. He will also make and distribute a clean copy of the deadlines for stages of the project. In large groups that must meet frequently outside of class, the recorder will want to find out everyone's schedules and publish them in some fashion.

Reporting Large Group Work

Sometimes your group will need to share its conclusions or papers with others. In these situations, the entire group may participate in the presentation or the recorder may report for the group. He can read his notes better than anyone else, and he has concentrated on watching the group work through the assignment. As a reporter, he will want to present the group's solution to the problem and describe briefly how they arrived at it. If there are one or two individuals who strongly disagreed with the group's decision, then the reporter should also present their views.

ANTICIPATING PROBLEMS AND THEIR SOLUTIONS

No project ever goes completely smoothly, and it is worth anticipating problems that you may face. Although this sounds a bit negative, anticipating problems will make the difficulties seem less disorienting when they arise. Instead of saying, "Oh, no, what are we going to do?" you can say, "Well, we anticipated this—now let's deal with it." Discussing potential problems gives you a sense of control over them. If you run into difficulty, it is not because you have failed but because difficulties are inevitable. Also, talking about problems lets the entire group set standards for itself. If you decide that a group member who does not do her work will be dropped from the group, then everyone knows that they must do their work. And if someone slacks off and is removed from the group, the action will seem less personal than procedural. We rarely take it personally if we get a speeding ticket. We know that we are not supposed to exceed the speed limit, and, if we do, we risk the consequences.

Sharing the Workload

The most aggravating group experiences that I have had involved individuals who either did not do their work or insisted on doing everything. You may find that one group member does not do the jobs assigned to her and so she slows down the group as a whole. She may be chronically late to meetings or with her assignments. Sometimes people who are unprepared pull the rest of the group off track when they ask irrelevant questions. In these situations, it is important to know why someone is not pulling her weight. Perhaps she has been ill. Perhaps she had to work overtime for several nights. Perhaps she is lazy or just doesn't care. The group will want to define their response to someone who does not do the work. Usually, the group will first discuss the problem openly, warning the individual and reminding her of the importance of each individual's contribution to the final project. If the person has been ill, can she switch tasks so that she can work more at the end of the project, when her energy has returned? If the individual is just not willing to work, most groups will warn her, then drop her from the group, reassigning her jobs to those who remain. In a classroom, this action is fairly serious since it means that the student will not be able to complete her work. Therefore, you should try to accommodate people's different work habits and their special needs so that they can complete their work before you decide that they just cannot continue to be part of the team. On the other hand, waiting too long to remove someone from the team may slow everyone down and destroy group morale and momentum.

At the other end of the spectrum are people who do too much: the bully and the willing martyr. The bully dominates the group by talking all the time and insisting that her ideas shape the group's work. She will not compromise. Your group may also have a willing martyr, someone who takes on the bulk of the work simply to "serve" the group, to make the group work go "smoothly." This is the kind of person who is always ready to say "I'll do it" when no one else volunteers. Before you know it, the martyr has more than he can do and so he fails to complete his work, does a poor job, or gets frustrated and angry at the group for exploiting him. Again, you want to know why these people act this way. Does the bully think that she is smarter and so is "saving" the group from its own ignorance? Does the martyr simply want to be liked? If you know why people act the way that they do, you can fashion a response to them. Since both of these problems involve people doing too much rather than too little, it is usually not too hard to get them to relax.

Keeping the Process Moving Along

Although everyone is working equally hard, some group processes will get stalled in details and justifications. Most of the time, these groups need a stronger leader who can direct discussion more efficiently. If this occurs, talk about the problem, and, if you need a new leader, appoint one. If the group works hard but gets nowhere, soon its members will lose their enthusiasm. This problem is, at least, easy to spot. When the project timetable shows that the group is lagging, then you must decide whether the timetable is unrealistic or your procedures are inefficient.

Dealing with Problems as a Group

If you have trouble in a traditional class, you often look to the teacher to solve it. He will tell you how to proceed if the library does not have a book or if someone is interfering with your work in some way. In collaborative learning, it is important that the group solve its own problems as much as possible. Obviously, the teacher is there if you need advice, but solving your own problems is part of group work.

If your group has difficulties with group dynamics, the best remedy is to bring the problem out into the open quickly. Frustrations that are not voiced can fester. The sooner a potential problem is identified, the sooner it can be addressed. And it is easier to remedy problems in their early stages than later on. As you talk about problems, be specific. Don't say, "Someone isn't doing their work." You may make "innocent" people feel guilty, and everyone will wonder who you're accusing. Similarly, don't say, "I just can't work with Larry." Be specific about the problem. Is it that you cannot find time to work together? Or, is it that Larry is not prepared? Finally, as the group discusses how to respond to a situation, look forward, not backward. The goal is to solve the problem from this point on, not to bemoan the situation or degrade the individual responsible for it. Don't think about punishment, but about solutions. Can you change the situation? If not, then how will the group proceed?

One easy way to discover problems in group dynamics is to undertake a group study like that recommended in the following exercise. Although such studies may seem quite artificial, they help groups see how they are working well or poorly. This exercise is also an interesting writing assignment since any group observer must choose words very carefully in order to represent the group's actions as accurately as possible. It is important for groups who work together on several projects to take time to study the group and improve the way its members interact.

Group Study Exercise.   Select either a group member or an outsider to serve as observer. This person will watch the group work for one full working session — not participating in the group, but just watching. The observer should take notes on behaviors as a recorder would, but in greater detail. Look especially at how individuals interact. How often does each group member speak? For how long? Who agreed with whom? If a debate developed, who seemed to speak most strongly for each side? After the group session is over, the observer will write a report describing the group's dynamics, choosing words carefully, and distinguishing her reactions from her observations.

The group will then read this report and discuss it. Are you surprised by what the observer saw? Is there anything that you want to change? What strengths does the group have?

Variation.   This exercise can be done by many people at once. For example, one group can observe and describe the behavior of another group at work. When more than one person observes a group, you can compare the observers' reports to see how individuals perceive the same actions differently. Again the group that has been observed will want to discuss the collection of observers' reports.

EVALUATING GROUP WORK

As I have already said, grades often seem inappropriate for collaborative work. Collaboration encourages you to take risks and speak honestly, while grades judge you in often baffling ways. If your school uses grades as the currency of the classroom, however, it is important that this collaborative work be evaluated. It is meaningful work. At some point the teacher will probably give you grades, but you and your group should also learn how to evaluate yourselves in this class.

In collaborative learning, you will find that your small group or the class as a whole may discuss criteria for evaluating a particular assignment. You will want to consider the qualities that will define a successful project, and you will also want to discuss how individual contributions and group products will be judged. Depending on the project, you and the teacher may decide to evaluate only the individual work completed by each group member and to assign individual grades. Or you may want the teacher to read or listen to a group report and give everyone the same grade for it. These decisions will rest in part on how autonomous the group members are.

Sometimes the teacher may ask individuals or the group as a whole to report on their relative success. In that case, a group study like the one described on p. 39 may answer the teacher's needs. She just wants to know if the work was equitably distributed. She is also interested in individuals' strengths and weaknesses. A group study or even an informal evaluation of the group will tell the teacher what she needs to discuss with the entire class or with a particular student about group dynamics. A team's self-evaluation is often the teacher's only window into the group process.

Keeping a Work Log

In order to study the group process or to record contributions made by each team member, some people keep a personal work log. This is a kind of diary, including notes from meetings, individual assignments, and reflections on the project and on your own work. This kind of log is especially helpful if your teacher asks you to evaluate either individual group members or the project as a whole. You know who did what when, and you can base your judgments on fact. Be sure that you clearly differentiate facts ("Vasanti was not at the meeting") from your opinions ("Vasanti is lazy"). These logs also let you record and reflect on your own work in a group. At the end of the semester, you may want to look back and see how you have grown and changed. The problems that obsessed you in the first few group projects may seem trivial by the end of the course.

INDIVIDUAL ACCOUNTABILITY

In this chapter, I have focused on how individuals can work together well in a group, how they can collaborate effectively. Some of you may find this advice obvious, while others of you may be wondering how you are going to keep it all in your head at once. Talking about group dynamics is a bit like talking about how to do the rhumba. It is much harder to describe than to do, and, as you do it, it will quickly become intuitive.

But I want to end with a reminder that groups are composed of individuals. Although this book will concentrate on group activities, you should remember that each individual is responsible for contributing to the group effort. If you cannot do the job assigned to you by the group, let them know so that the entire group is not held up while you complete your work. I said in the first chapter that this book will force you to become active. Let me add now that it will also force you to become responsible — not only to the teacher, but also to other class members who will be relying on you (as you rely on them) to complete assignments.

Exercise on Individual Response to Group Work.   Keep a personal journal recording ways in which your group or groups work. At the end of each work session, write an entry about how the session went and how you felt about your participation. You may also want to note anything new that you learned about working with other people. After you have completed several entries, you can use this journal as evidence for a short essay either describing how groups work or making recommendations on how your group could work better.

Self-Evaluation Exercise.   As an individual, make two lists of three items each, one headed "Good things that I do in groups" and the other "Bad things that I do in groups." Put these lists aside. Get together with your team, and divide into two subgroups, one group that will solve a problem and the other that will observe. Pair up so that each observer can study one of the discussants. Here is the problem that the group must discuss:

> *A poor man whose wife is critically ill needs to purchase medicine for her, but he has no money and no insurance to do so. He breaks into the pharmacy one night and steals the medicine, saving his wife's life. Should we consider him to be a criminal or not?*

After 15 minutes, the observers rejoin the group and share notes with the persons they each observed. Did the observer see what you thought were your strengths and weaknesses? Does she react to you as you expected, or did she interpret your hesitancy to speak as careful consideration of the issues? Now reverse the roles so that the participants become the observers, and repeat the exercise.

SUGGESTED PAPER TOPICS

1. Complete the exercise on analyzing assumptions (p. 26) and write a report on the values implicit in the audience, the host, and the guests for this talk show. Be as specific as possible. Draw upon your discussions as a group, but go beyond them as well.

2. Write a short essay evaluating how your group or groups have functioned so far this semester. Does the group work better on certain kinds of assignments? What kinds of problems have you faced and how have you dealt with them? Write this paper in the style of an interim report to your supervisor (in this case, probably your teacher).

3. Think about your family situation either when you were growing up or in your new family if you are married or have children of your own. How did your family negotiate differences? Focus on a specific decision that the family had to make. Describe your family's decision-making process, demonstrating the principles by which they negotiated differences.

4. Define the idea of "an author" for a piece of writing. Must an author's ideas be totally "new"? If not, how do we distinguish between an author's ideas and the ideas that she read or talked about with various people? What does it mean to be the author of a new idea?

5. Select a topic on which you are an authority — choosing a college, the medieval priesthood, rock music, computers, or whatever. Then identify two different sorts of readers who might be interested in aspects of the topic. Think of a question that both readers might have about this topic. For example, both your parents and your friends might want to know how you decided to end a relationship or to attend a particular college. Write a one- to two-page paper, answering this question for both of your two audiences. That is, you will be writing the same general paper twice, but gearing your writing to different audiences.

CHAPTER
3

A CASE
IN POINT:
REVISING WITH
PEER RESPONSE

Having explored how collaboration works, you are now ready to put your collaborative skills to work. The previous chapters have described the process of solving problems or doing research as a group. Probably this work will culminate in some kind of writing. So, let's examine how you can work with others while you write. Basically, there are two kinds of collaborative writing: helping one another to revise (discussed in this chapter), and creating a paper with other writers (discussed in the next chapter).

I will focus first on revising because it is the most common collaborative writing activity for individual authors. Even writers who work in complete isolation most of the time try to get feedback from others. Revising alone is never as productive as revising collaboratively. For this reason, in school you will often be asked to collaborate as you revise. As you write, you discover ideas and then put them into language so that someone else can understand what you're thinking. You write what you think and then shape it for a reader. This shaping is revision. To revise well, you need feedback from a reader. You need to know what the reader understands or does not understand and why.

Unfortunately, some people associate revision with failure. They have been told too many tall tales of famous authors writing brilliant works in one quick draft. For example, Samuel Taylor Coleridge claimed that he wrote "Kubla Khan," one of the greatest British poems, in just a few minutes after waking from a dream. Few people believe this story, and, even if it were true, it would be memorable only because it is so unusual. We have a myth that good writers don't revise. That myth is simply not true. But it is reinforced in school when teachers request revised papers only from those students whose essays were inadequate. In school, some students see revision as punishment. In fact, teachers know that all writing is revised. They expect everyone to draft and redraft their work, and they request additional revisions only from those who seem to have done too little revising.

People also confuse revision with editing, in which the writer checks word choice and grammar. But revising literally means "reseeing." When you revise, you look at your work through new eyes. You question your assumptions and the connections between your ideas. You reconsider your conclusions. You move paragraphs, create transitions, cut chunks of prose, add evidence, and, yes, consider word choice and grammar. But when you are revising a completed draft, you want to look first at large issues like defining your central point, before you consider commas. After all, if you looked at sentence-level concerns first, you could spend 15 minutes correcting the grammar in a paragraph that you later cut because it was irrelevant.

Revising takes courage. You need to believe that by daring to think about what you are saying and how you are saying it, you will improve your writing. You need to be critical of your prose in order to improve it. Revising also takes time. In planning your schedule, be sure to leave lots of time to rework your material and let your work "cool," to get some distance from it. It is very hard to revise work that you have just written. When I am writing a paper, I know so well what I *intend* to say that I cannot see what I have really said. I cannot even listen carefully to readers' responses to my work until I've put it away for a while. Sometimes I have to wait a week or two before I can see my own work with a reader's eyes.

THE VALUE OF PEER RESPONSE

Professional writers call on their colleagues to read and comment on their work. Journalists show their work to other journalists. As I write this text in a computer room, a geologist sitting next to me is sharing his work with a colleague, asking her what is unclear in a certain paragraph. Since you are a student, your colleagues are your friends and classmates. They are your peer readers. They can read your work and tell you what they hear, where they are excited about your ideas, where they are confused, and so on. Unfortunately, too many students never receive this kind of feedback. The only response they get to their writing is a teacher's evaluation. Teachers' comments are unquestionably valuable, but they are quite different from the kind of response that a reader can give you. Teachers evaluate a finished piece of work. They judge the merits and failures of your writing, offering you a picture of how your work is progressing. Classmates respond while you are in the midst of writing; they become your consultants, and sometimes even your allies. You solicit their response, listen carefully, choose what you can use, and revise accordingly. Because you get comments from your friends and classmates as you are writing, you can act immediately on what you learn from them. The teacher's comments will then tell you how successful you've been.

When I first started teaching, I spent a lot of time responding to my students' drafts, trying to give the writers feedback while they were writing. For hours I pored over papers, making suggestions, and then I waited eagerly to see the result. But when I read the final drafts, I saw that too often students had followed my advice blindly. As I had suggested, they added a detail or rearranged the paper's sections, but they obviously hadn't known why. They hadn't learned anything from my comments but secretarial skills. I realized that my students felt obligated to follow my directions. In short, I was writing their papers for them and then grading myself. As a student, I remember feeling obliged to follow my teachers' comments in a similar way. After all, if the teacher was going to grade my work, why not write it the way he wanted it? When people are judging my work, I feel that I must conform to their sense of what I should say. But when I work with a colleague to revise my writing, we negotiate the meaning. Talking with someone, I can clarify what I mean and probe my reader's responses.

Sometimes when I ask my students to exchange papers and give each other formal or informal feedback, I have the feeling that some students resent it. I can almost hear them saying, "What a lazy teacher! Why are we doing *her* work?" These students do not realize that they can give each other a very different kind of feedback than I can give them. They are not "doing my work"; they are doing a different kind of work.

Not only can your classmates make in-process comments, but they also have a different type of authority than the teacher. They speak the same language as you do, and you share standards with them. These are the people you will live and work with for the rest of your lives. They are the people who will read and evaluate your writing when you are on the job. As a result, many of my students say that they respond differently when a peer says that their writing is unclear than when I tell them that. They believe that their classmates respond more honestly than I do.

There are, of course, times when a teacher may ask you to check each other's papers based on some specific criteria for an assignment. She may ask you, for example, to be sure that there are no fragments or run-ons in the paper. Although this kind of evaluation is much closer to what a teacher does when she reads your papers, reading someone else's work in this way will help you spot errors that may occur in your own work. It is always easier to find errors in someone else's work than in your own.

Even when you feel as if you are judging a classmate's work, your task is still quite different from a teacher's. You may evaluate paragraph unity or soundness of argument, but because your comments reach the writer while she is still working on the piece, you are not judging a final product. You are working together to improve the writer's work. In writing this kind of comment, you must be especially careful to be honest and not parrot a teacher's voice. If you find that you are making comments in order to impress the teacher, you are probably no longer positioning yourself as the writer's consultant. Your comments should always be designed to benefit the writer, not please the teacher. You must also think not simply of what's right or wrong, but *how* the writing can be improved. If the argument is not sound, should the writer start over again, abandon the argument, write to a different audience, or gather more supporting evidence?

I know that some students dread exchanging their work with their classmates because they are afraid that their classmates will be more critical than the teacher. Some of my students worry that their classmates will laugh at them. To avoid this kind of problem, your teacher will guide you through the process of peer response very carefully. You will need to learn a new way to respond to each other's work, one that is quite different from the kind of remarks that a teacher makes. If you read each other's papers as a teacher would, you will simply duplicate a teacher's effort. If, however, you work from your special position as a peer commenting on writing in process, you can complement the teacher's evaluation.

Stages of Peer Feedback

Peer feedback can be useful at many different stages of the writing process. When you are just beginning to pull ideas together, quickly explaining those ideas orally to a classmate or friend can help clarify them or lead you to discover new ideas. I remember that my friends in college always dreaded talking to me when I was writing a paper because I would want to rehearse my ideas with them while they were trying to swallow the cafeteria food. At this stage, you need to have the listener ask questions that address content and request more information. My favorite listeners in college asked questions like "But what about . . ." or "Is that like . . . ?" Having a conversation at the start of the writing process can also help you envision your readers.

Once the work is written in some form, readers can give more extensive feedback. But before a writer and reader can converse meaningfully, they need to share their assumptions about the content of the piece. The first task for the reader, therefore, is to summarize the paper. Considering questions like the following can be helpful.

> "What is this essay about?"
> "What is the writer's opinion?"
> "Why is the writer writing this paper?"

If the reader and writer disagree about the paper's content, they should try to reach agreement without bullying one another. If they cannot agree quickly, then they should settle for understanding each other's points of view. Remember that you should not argue the "correctness" of each others' interpretations. If the writer meant to say a particular thing, then she meant to say it. If the reader heard something else, then that is what he heard. It is the writer's job to see how the reader was misled and to make necessary changes.

Here is a transcript from Karen Spear's book *Sharing Writing* that shows how summarizing and questioning a writer's main idea can help that writer clarify and extend her point. In this case, Audrey has written a draft for her education course that describes a three-week plan of study she might give her students. After the group has read the draft and Audrey has summarized it, Karen tries to understand the details of Audrey's teaching plan.

KAREN: OK. So [you're going to ask the students to] participate in group discussion this whole year?

AUDREY: No, they . . . No. No. This isn't the whole year. This is for the unit [of study]. OK?

KAREN: OK.

AUDREY: Now, uh . . .

KAREN: [But] the unit is for the whole year? The first page [of the paper] is [about] the whole year. What you plan on doing.

AUDREY: Uh huh.

KAREN: What you want them to do . . . no?

AUDREY: Yeah. That's what I want 'em to do. I want 'em to have responsibilities, you know, I'd get — I never thought of it that way.

KAREN: I don't understand.

AUDREY: OK.

KAREN: I got the idea that you wanted to do this the whole year long and these were some of the things they were gonna do throughout the year.

AUDREY: No. All right. The overall objectives will be the whole year type objectives. OK? Maybe.

KAREN: OK, then, what the students are expected to do in the unit . . .

AUDREY: . . . in the unit is in these two weeks. It may end up being a three-week unit because there's a lot of stuff in there.

KAREN: OK. But the I AM book [that they will each write] is [for] the whole year, isn't it?

AUDREY: Um, it will be a continuous process so they will keep adding to it. I'd like 'em to all have file folders of their writing.

In order for Audrey and Karen to discuss this draft, they first need to share an understanding of Audrey's basic proposal. As Karen questions Audrey, you can see her making distinctions between year-long projects and the subtasks that will be part of this two-week period of study. Karen is asking questions, but she is not leading Audrey to answers. She paraphrases what she heard: "I got the idea that you wanted. . . ." Although there is some confusion here, the two women do not argue or debate. They work together to reach a common understanding.

Once you understand how each of you reads the paper, you can discuss essay-level concerns like soundness of argument and organization. A reader might examine a section of the paper, write a question, and then go on to the next section. This transcript of the reader's questions can help the writer organize the work. The reader might also title or label each section of the paper. Like the transcript of the reader's questions, the reader's labels will help the writer to see how the reader is reading. These concerns may seem more "subjective" than giving "objective" feedback on grammar and mechanics, but there is no reason to discuss sentences and words until the ideas are in order.

After larger concerns have been discussed, some writers need to work on the piece alone for a while, revising it before getting more feedback. Other writers may want sentence-level feedback right away. When and if readers and writers talk about grammar and mechanics, they will find it more useful to focus on repeated errors rather than isolated ones. Going through a paper line by line may seem thorough, but it can quickly get tedious. Sometimes, when a reader points to a writer's sentence-level errors, the writer becomes little more than a secretary for the reader, taking down his corrections.

Of course, the procedures that you follow will depend largely on whether you are working with written comments or a face-to-face conference. They will also change if a writer is receiving feedback from one reader or many. When you work together in pairs, reading and commenting on each other's work, you may have more of a sense of responsibility toward each other. Talking about your papers will probably be more efficient. In a larger group, where two or three readers provide feedback to a single writer, conversation may be more difficult to direct, but the writer will be assured that one reader's response is not idiosyncratic. Sometimes it is too easy for a writer to dismiss an individual reader's confusion, saying, "Anyone else would have understood me." With a group, this is more difficult.

Exercise on Responding as a Reader.   Individually, read the following student paper and write a quick, one-sentence summary of its content. Then, in groups of two, three, or four students, compare your summaries of the paper. How similar are they? How do they differ and why? Are there instances of a reader's bias shaping her response? Are there places in the text that are ambiguous? Be prepared to report your discussion to the class as a whole.

Topic: *Describe a tradition with which you are acquainted, whether a national, ethnic, family, or personal one. As part of your description you should discuss what significance this tradition supposedly has. A good paper would also consider whether the tradition retains any significance, or has become merely hollow ritual, and why. (You may, of course, include your own reasons for accepting or rejecting the tradition.) Focus your attention on only one tradition for this paper.*

I come from a Polish-Mexican background. In my family there are many traditions because of the great differences between the two cultures. I will focus on one special Polish tradition and that is the breaking of Oplatki.

The breaking of Oplatki is always done on Christmas Eve before the main meal in the evening. There is usually a large crowd because all of the relatives from my mother's side gather together this night to celebrate Christmas.

Oplatki is a thin wafer-like edible food shaped in a rectangle and sometimes stamped with a Nativity scene or other Christmas scene. It is white usually but can be tinted pink. Each person receives a sizeable portion of Oplatki. After prayers are said the breaking begins. Each person there goes to every relative and breaks a piece of his Oplatki. In turn, that relative breaks a piece off the other person's. It is then eaten. After this, the two people show some sign of affection toward each other by a kiss or a hug. This goes on til everyone has given a piece of Oplatki to everyone there.

This tradition is also Catholic. Its significance is that we should all be brothers, <u>especially</u> united since we are in the same family. It is done on Christmas because Christ's birth symbolizes the beginning or starting over again. The best way to start a new year is to get rid of old grudges, settle differences, and be on good terms with one another. The bread is like a symbolic Holy Communion. We all participate and are therefore united in some way.

After taking part and observing this tradition this past Christmas, I realized that it is still very significant and important to almost everyone. There are seldom arguments or long-term grudges in our family and this tradition may have something to do with this fact. The younger children in our family also participate in this and I think it is good for them to be raised on this tradition.

My own reasons for accepting this is partly because I was raised in the tradition but mainly because I can see the good that it does and can appreciate having my relatives as friends.

Exercise on Group Response.   Read the following paper on "Richardson Hall." As an individual, respond to these questions in writing:

Read the first paragraph; where do you expect the piece to go?

Now read the rest of the paper. Were your expectations fulfilled? If not, what is the rest of the paper about?

What is the main idea of the piece (in one sentence)?

Divide the piece into sections and label them. Are there any irrelevant sections? Are there redundant sections?

What writing strategy would you recommend that the writer follow at this point (e.g., cut paragraphs apart and reshuffle, send the paper through a spell checker)?

Once you have completed your individual response to this piece, form groups of three or four students. Read your responses to these questions and try to reach consensus on the most useful responses. Imagine that the writer is a part of your group. When you are done, write out three things that you discovered about peer response through this process.

IN DEFENSE OF RICHARDSON HALL

Richardson Hall is an important structure on the campus because of its beauty and functionality. It would be a careless mistake for the University Building Commission to have the building demolished to make way for a new dorm. It is important for the University to respect and maintain the historical buildings that add character and originality to the campus. Richardson Hall is not only a building with such character, in addition it provides a unique atmosphere for its inhabitants that cannot be found in other housing facilities.

Built in the early 1920's, Richardson Hall reflects a period of architecture that maintained a respect for details. This detail could only be achieved through long hard hours of labor. Craftsmanship is an important feature of the old building. The existing external structure is made of carefully laid bricks that are now different shades of yellow, orange, and brown because of the years of weathering that have occurred. Arches and oddly-shaped windows appear all over the four story building. It is a beautiful example of Eastern architecture in that respect; the curves remind you of the boat designer.

The interior is truly extraordinary because convenient, modern facilities have been installed. The contrast between old and new styles within provide the inhabitants with a rich living space. The interior is luxurious-looking in a sense. The detailed plasterwork and excessively intricate fixtures are pleasant in comparison to the seemingly cold characteristics of modern-day, economic-minded furnishings and designs.

When viewed as an entity of a larger community of buildings in the area, Richardson is pleasantly distinct. The building is well-kept and attractive on the outside. It is well-placed; it sits facing the main campus on the corner of Thayer and Manning, right next to the purposeful and modern Science Library. The two provide an interesting contrast. Richardson Hall is a symbol of the past that adds to the character of the school, part of a composite that infers progress and respect.

Inhabitants of Richardson Hall find it a preferable living space because of its relatively small size and special character. Nine separate, multi-inhabitant dwellings make up Richardson's living facilities. The individual unit is akin to a household because of the number of rooms within; the people are provided with a fertile opportunity to develop a character for their living space. Ginny Goss, a senior who lives in Richardson, said "Living in Richardson is great. I feel like I'm right at home." The familiarity Richardson produces is rare on the campus. The University should try to preserve the building in the students interest. It is necessary for the University to have a measure of diversity in housing so the students will remain diverse.

Richardson houses convenient game and laundry rooms that exceed standard, modern dorm facilities. It would be costly to re-create those luxuries in a modern dorm. In the rear of the building sets a sizeable grassy patch that allows occupants a "back yard." Students frequently walk their dogs in the space that remains lighted in the evenings. The building is one of the few dorms left on the campus where one can reasonably maintain a pet.

Demolishing Richardson would be a careless waste of a perfectly adequate housing facility. It is in generally good condition and has been maintained quite well. The

fire safety systems are modern and extensive. Accessible
fire escapes insure the safety of the building.

Richardson Hall occupies a central location in the
campus. It provides the campus with the historical depth
that must be maintained. The University's past is critical
in terms of preserving an atmosphere unique to the school.
Richardson Hall is a clear indicator of that past. It is
also a unique and charming facility for upperclassmen to
live in. The rooms are spacious and comfortable and offer
students a necessary option in the opportunities for
campus housing. A new dorm should be constructed in an
area that does not directly interfere with the
preservation of the historical University buildings.
Richardson, like great works of art, must be preserved
carefully because once they are destroyed, they are
irretrievable.

Exercise on Oral Feedback in a Group.   In groups of three or four
students, select one person to read a paper she is working on and will be
revising. The writer will read the paper aloud while the others in the
group listen and take notes. Then, each member of the group should
offer her a summary of the paper, a description of how he responded to
it, and suggestions for revising strategies. If you like, use the list of
questions in the previous exercise to guide your discussion. The writer
should take notes. When your discussion is complete, each individual
should write down three things that worked well for the group and
three problems that the group encountered. Discuss these responses
and be prepared to report to the class as a whole.

PREPARING YOUR DRAFT FOR A READER

Asking classmates or friends to read your first, halting draft may only frus-
trate them. Before you know it, you will run out of people who are willing to
read and respond to your work. Before you give a "final draft" to a reader,
you should revise it on your own.

When you prepare your draft for a reader, you need to alternate between being a reader and being yourself—the writer. That is, you must ask
and answer your own questions. Before you reread the piece, picture your
audience clearly. Hear your voice "talking" to that audience. I find it very
useful to read my text aloud. Hearing the text distances it for me and makes

my reader seem more real. The more clearly you envision your reader, the more vividly you will see her nod, frown, chuckle, or furrow her brow in confusion. If you have been writing on a word processor, this is the time to work from a printout. You will need to see how parts of the paper fit together, and flipping from one page to another is easier on paper than on a screen. Just changing the presentation of your words from lights on a computer screen to ink on paper will help you see your writing with new eyes.

As you rework your draft, concentrate first on clarifying ideas and arguments. You want to be sure that your ideas are clearly represented in the paper so that your reader can respond to them. As you revise, begin by reading the whole essay, asking questions like "What am I saying? Where is it clear and where unclear?" You may find the main point is stated in one sentence. Or it may be implicit in your essay as a whole. Underline or write out the main idea so that you can refer to it quickly as you continue to revise.

Next, read the essay in chunks to see if each part of the argument is fully developed and connected to the next point that you make. I often find it helpful to draw lines across the page, marking where sections of my work appear to begin and end. Then I label each section with a word, phrase, or sentence. Sometimes I think of these phrases as titles for the sections (like subheadings in a report or an outline). When I label each chunk of a paper with full phrases or sentences, I can read them to see if they sound like a summary of the paper. Reading these labels tells me quickly whether or not the piece flows. If you find this process cumbersome, try writing an abstract of your work. Can you reduce the piece to a paragraph that represents your main idea and its development as the paper progresses?

After you have made any necessary changes to fill in holes in your argument or delete irrelevant digressions, you may need to re-outline the piece or write a new abstract so that you can check your new structure. The notes and outlines that you produce as you revise will also be useful as you discuss your paper with a reader. The last step in revising on your own is to read the paper aloud to yourself, listening for stylistic problems (repeated words, endless sentences, etc.) that your eye could not see.

Remember that all your changes may not be improvements. As I revise my drafts on a word processor, I usually copy and save the old text before changing it. That way, if I decide later that I prefer an early draft of some section, I still have the text available to me. It is also easier to cut a text if you know that the words you deleted are still saved somewhere.

Perhaps the best way to demonstrate how revision can shape prose before it goes to a reader is to show you a text at various stages of the writing process. The following paragraph is taken from this chapter. As I revised it, you can see how different shapes emerged and the style became more direct. The versions are presented in chronological order.

   A. Revision, then is usually most concentrated after a draft is completed. Unfortunately, some people associate revision with failure. They have been told too many stories of great authors writing brilliant works in one quick draft. We have a myth that good writers don't revise. That myth is simply not true. But it is reinforced in school when the teacher requests revised papers only from those students whose essays were inadequate. In school, some students see revision as punishment. In fact, the teacher knows that all writing is revised. She expects everyone to draft and redraft their work, and she requests additional revisions only from those who seem to have done too little revising.

B. Unfortunately, some people associate revision with failure. They have been told too many tall tales of great authors writing brilliant works in one quick draft. For example, they may have heard the tale of Samuel Taylor Coleridge supposedly waking from a dream and writing "Kubla Khan" in a few minutes. Great gymnasts and pianists make their work seem easy, even though it is still hard. Some great writers want to make their work seem easy too — even though it isn't. We have a myth that good writers don't revise.

That myth is simply not true. But it is reinforced in school when teachers request revised papers only from those students whose essays were inadequate. In school, some students see revision as punishment. In fact, teachers know that all writing is revised. They expect everyone to draft and redraft their work, and they request additional revisions only from those who seem to have done too little revising.

C. Unfortunately, some people associate revision with failure. They have been told too many tall tales of famous authors writing brilliant works in one quick draft. For example, Samuel Taylor Coleridge claimed that he wrote "Kubla Khan," one of the greatest British poems, in just a few minutes after waking from a dream. Few people believe this story, and, even if it were true, it would be memorable only because it is so unusual. We have a myth that good writers don't revise. That myth is simply not true. But it is reinforced in school when teachers request revised papers only from those students whose essays were inadequate. In school, some students see revision as punishment. In fact, teachers know that all writing is revised. They expect everyone to draft and redraft their work, and they request additional revisions only from those who seem to have done too little revising.

Once you have initially revised your work, be sure that your reader's copy is as clean as possible so that she has no trouble deciphering your writing. Some teachers recommend that students read their papers aloud to each other during peer review sessions, especially if writers are getting feedback from several students in a group situation. But I think that you will benefit more from having your readers actually read your work. Speech is different from writing, and most papers were meant to be read, not heard.

Only if your paper is at a very early stage would I suggest that you read it aloud to your reviewers.

In preparing to give your work to a reader, work hard enough on it so that you have some commitment to its ideas and expressions. But do not work so hard that you are unwilling to revise it. Usually, when you exchange papers, you will want to tell the reader what stage you are at, so that she knows what kinds of comments to make. I often ask writers to tell their readers what they would do if they had 24 hours to work on this paper. This helps define what the writer is willing to consider revising. Other useful things to tell your readers are what you see as your main idea, what the assignment is (if it's not clear), which parts of the paper you like best, and which you like least. In order to direct the reader's attention to your concerns, be sure to give the reader two to four questions that you would like to have her address. For example, you may wonder if your introduction is too long, or if your example on page 5 makes sense. You may be worried that you have included too much plot summary or too little. Often, you need suggestions for how to cut the paper or lengthen it.

If you have a chance to meet and talk with your readers as part of your revising process, you should lead the discussion or develop the questions. Again, this reminds you and your readers that their feedback is designed to suit your needs. A conference is your time and you know what you need. Asking questions or leading a discussion requires you to think about how you will use the reader's response. Are you willing to reconsider your main idea? Or do you want to fix up the style? Just like the reader, you need to have a clear agenda when you begin the process of peer review.

Exercise on Preparing a Draft for a Reader.   The following is a brief paper written in response to the assignment:

> *Arthur Koestler claims that aliens in science fiction can be "too alien to be true." In that case, he says, "without an act of identification, of intimate understanding, there is no art, only a thrill of curiosity which soon yields to boredom." Agree or disagree with this statement.*

Read the paper and revise it. Then, in a group discuss what you liked about the original piece and what you wanted to change. Compare your revisions. Did the members of the group build on the same or different aspects of the original piece? Did some people focus on the argument and others on sentences and grammar? Note your natural tendencies in rewriting as an individual. As a group, discuss the strategies you used to revise the work. Did some of you cut and paste? Others read aloud? What did you focus on first? Be prepared to discuss your successful strategies with the whole class.

Curiosity Never Dies

The lack of understanding a person, or concept, should present a challenge to anyone with the most slightly curious mind. Therefore, this writer must disagree with Arthur Koestler's claim that aliens in science fiction can be "too alien to be true." The curious mind of a truly inquisitive being is never wholly satisfied.

Given a situation in which an alien's ways or thought pattern are totally incomprehensible, a challenge is made to which one should never give way. Boredom is merely a state of mind for those who have given up thinking, or have stopped pondering a particularly difficult problem. One can honestly say that the thrill of curiosity that Koestler talks about should be sparked and fanned by the idea of an alien "too alien to be true."

Man responds to concepts strange and new to him. Creatures with six eyes, four arms, antennae and a tail would create a mixture of emotions within any man. But one must admit that curiosity, the need to know more, would motivate a person, possible second only to fear.

Drawing from what has previously been said, one must conclude that curiosity is the spark of our imagination. Curiosity maintains within us a constant circle of thought. This constant mill of thought makes man what he is and keeps him moving forward. "Too alien to be true? This is doubtful. After all, it is said that variety is the spice of life.

Exercise Comparing Peer Revision and Self-Directed Revision. After you have completed an assignment for this course, copy it and give the copy to your partner. Read and revise your partner's paper as if it were your own. Make his arguments as clear as you can. Then, look back at your own paper and revise it once more. Do you feel differently when you revise your own work than when you revise someone else's? Is the process different? Which process do you prefer? Now, show your partner how you revised his paper. Did you make different changes than he did when he revised on his own? Did you understand his intentions? Look at how he revised your paper and ask the same questions. Write a brief report from this experience to hand in to your teacher.

THE ROLE OF THE PEER READER

The most important thing to remember when you are responding to a classmate's writing is that you are the writer's ally. Treat the text as if it were a professional essay—don't hunt for error. Sit back, read the piece, and then respond. As you can see, in some ways being a peer reader requires no expertise. A teacher must have criteria to inform her judgment; a reader only needs to make a good faith effort to understand the text and then report his experience accurately. He may actually know very little about the subject being discussed. Many professional writers rely on friends and spouses as their first readers. My husband, a mathematician and computer scientist, often reads my articles on writing or on theatre before anyone else does. In fact, he is the first reader for this book. I do not expect him to judge the quality of my research or to determine if my ideas are fresh. I only want to know if he hears me saying what I think that I have said. This is the role you will play as a peer reader.

During the process of peer feedback, it is important for the writer and reader to cooperate rather than to compete. The goal is to work together, not to work at the expense of each other. I have seen students who thought that the purpose of peer response was for readers to show their expertise by finding every possible error in the writer's work. They felt that their grade would improve if they demonstrated their superiority by identifying as many errors as they could. This kind of relationship between the writer and reader is combative and counterproductive. Would you want to work with someone whose primary interest was in making you look foolish? When I say that the writer and reader should cooperate, though, I do not mean that you should offer each other empty praise. Some of my students are afraid to hurt each other's feelings, and so they simply tell each other that their papers are "fine." This kind of feedback wastes both the writer's and the reader's time. When someone tells me that my work is "fine" and gives me no details, I assume that he thinks I am incapable of doing any better. In other words, I feel slighted.

If you are honest and respect one another, you will be able to give thorough and straightforward feedback to one another. To provide each other with good feedback, you need to trust each other. Remember that students who regularly get A's on their papers can benefit from comments by students who regularly get C's on their work. Great novelists, playwrights, and essayists often worked closely with readers and editors whose names have already been forgotten. On the other hand, if you have trouble writing, cherish the opportunity to get comments from people who have mastered the strange art of school writing. Do not be embarrassed to show them your work; they are not your judges but your co-workers. Learning how to give and take criticism from one's peers can be the most valuable lesson that you take from this course.

When you are responding as reader, you will summarize the paper that you read or find its main point. You may be asked to read the introduction and write down where you think the paper will go. You might locate places where you were lost or confused or angry or surprised. You could be asked to extend the argument of the paper, adding evidence or examples or related ideas. Or, you might be asked to write counterarguments or to describe images that the essay gave you. These are the kind of questions that you cannot be "wrong" in answering. Either you were surprised on page 3 or you were not. These questions are also useful because they are not clearly positive or negative. If you were surprised on page 3, you might have read something irrelevant, or you might have encountered a new and exciting idea.

Usually you will be asked to respond in writing to your classmates' essays. Written comments give the reader more time to consider her reactions and to word them carefully. They also preserve the reader's responses so that both the writer and the reader can refer to them later. If you are giving comments in writing, however, you must work extra hard to avoid imitating teacher's comments. Sometimes writing on a separate sheet of paper and not on the essay itself can help to remind you that you are a responding reader, not a teacher "correcting" a paper.

When I ask students to read each other's work, I usually ask them to respond to four or five questions. If I want them to act as peer readers (not evaluators), they complete the following form. I like the questions on this form because they ask the reader to believe in the writer's position as well as to doubt it. This combination expresses the reader's complex role of supporting the writer, while also responding rigorously to his work.

You will also notice that the form asks for each of your phone numbers and records the dates on which you exchanged papers. As you can imagine, it is very important that you and the writer be able to get in touch with each other. What if one of you became sick during the peer review process? How would you get papers back to each other? Having phone numbers can be very useful. Also, noting the dates on which papers are exchanged and returned records how punctual each of you is. Obviously, both writer and reader must respect deadlines and due dates so that you each have time to do your work.

Reader Response Form

Reader's Name _____   Author's Name _____

Phone _____   Phone _____

Date paper returned _____   Date paper received _____

The purpose of exchanging papers and providing comments on each other's work is three-fold. First, I know that you will become better readers of your own work if given a chance to read it "cold," having not seen it for several days. More important, I hope that this exercise will give you a model for constructive sharing of ideas. Because there will be a record of your exchanges, you should feel free to share without fear of cheating. Finally, I hope that by seeing several other papers from the class, you will gain a broader perspective on how these essay topics might be addressed.

Schedule

Exchange papers in class on Wednesday. Groups will meet briefly to plan the second exchange, to take place outside of class on Monday. Next Wednesday, you will submit your first version of the paper, the two reader's comment sheets, and your final draft. I will read and grade only the final draft.

For the Writer

Please answer the following questions BEFORE handing the paper to your reader.

1. If you had 24 more hours to work on this paper, what would you do?

2. What questions/issues would you like the readers to address? You can ask about specific arguments, style, evidence, interpretation, etc.

Continued

For the Reader

Read the paper once without worrying about these questions, then answer the questions, referring to the paper and rereading it as needed.

1. *Mirroring:* What is the main point of this paper? (Summarize in no more than three sentences.)

2. *Believing:* Accept the writer's point of view and try to extend the essay's argument — provide additional examples, suggest questions that might provoke further thought, discuss parallels.

Continued

3. *Doubting:* Provide counterevidence and counterarguments for the author. If you did not accept this argument, what objections might you raise? Are there other solutions or interpretations for this problem? Pursue one counterargument at length or suggest several concerns more briefly.

4. *Suggesting:* Based on your experience as a writer, what suggestions might you give the author? This is the time to warn the author if the paper merely repeats class discussion (however elegantly). This is also a chance to suggest revision tactics, remark on the essay's style, proportions, etc.

5. Respond to the author's questions above.

Giving Feedback in Conferences

Whether or not you write comments for each other, you will probably want to discuss the paper face to face at some point. The writer and the reader need time to understand each other more fully. The writer needs an opportunity to request clarification of the comments, try out revisions, and understand her reader's needs. The reader may find it easier to be specific when talking with the writer than when writing to her. In conferences, the reader can use his tone of voice to make his attitudes or opinions clear. For example, the statement "This was an interesting point" could be said and meant in several different ways. These conversations can also remind you that the paper is in process. Clearly the object of the discussion is to define a revision strategy for the writer. What should she do next? Focusing on revising and not judging past performance will emphasize that the writer and reader are allies, not opponents.

Face-to-face conferences work on many of the same principles as exchanging written comments. Look at this continuation of Audrey's conference that I cited earlier.

AUDREY: OK, so what I need to do, then, is just add more to my objectives, my overall objectives . . . examples . . .

KAREN: I don't know. I just read the paper that she [the teacher] gave me on revising and it seems like one of the main things professional writers do is that they try to grasp the form of what they mean.

AUDREY: Uh huh.

KAREN: . . . and put that in. But when you just have "students will identify their roles as learner," you don't really have a form, you're just saying . . .

AUDREY: You can't see it, can you?

KAREN: No.

AUDREY: OK.

KAREN: It needs to be bigger.

AUDREY: So, I need to put in *how's* on all my objectives, right?

LORI: It's real interesting to me how 2 follows 1, because 2 seems like that would come first.

AUDREY: Really?

LORI: Yeah. 'Cause it seems like you could look at "where do I fit in my family?" That's much easier to understand, that's much less abstract than "How do I fit in as a learner?" — I mean, you just don't think about that.

AUDREY: Maybe what I was doing, maybe what I could do is just take out the #2.

LORI: Yeah.

AUDREY: And, uh, go from, just add that on to #2? Would that be better?

LORI: Yeah — or, and, and change the wording "Translate this identity. . . .'' 'Cause it seems like identifying first with my family and all that comes first.

AUDREY: OK, Maybe that they will, uh . . .

LORI: 'Cause I really like how your ideas are developing.

In this section of the conference, Karen and Lori both act as readers, but they serve different functions. We saw earlier how the first thing that Karen and Audrey did was to establish the content of Audrey's draft. Now Karen is urging Audrey to expand her ideas; she is "believing" her and extending her ideas. Lori also acts as a reader, but she "doubts" Audrey, suggesting that students would find it easier to identify their family roles than their roles as learners.

It is clear from their tone and from Audrey's response that both Karen and Lori are on Audrey's side. They are acting as consultants for her. Consultants are, after all, called in for advice. They must take on the goals of their client. A consultant hired to advise a bank on its international expansion must accept the fact that the bank will expand globally. The consultant cannot recommend that the bank become a food store. Like a consultant, a peer reader must work from the writer's point of view, taking on the writer's position. Asking the writer to change her opinion on date rape or to write on violence in sports instead of modern warfare would be inappropriate. In these excerpts from the conference transcript, Audrey seems quite willing to take her readers' advice. But don't be surprised if all your suggestions are not accepted. This does not mean that you have failed, just that the writer has a different plan in mind. In fact, if we saw Audrey's final paper, we would probably find that she actually incorporated only a few of these suggestions. Others may have become obsolete as she revised.

As Eugene Gendlin remarks in his *Experiencing and the Creation of Meaning*, "Change in thinking does not occur as a result of talking, it occurs rather as one talks." Sitting face to face and discussing a paper may take more discipline than communicating through written comments, but it does allow people to change their minds. Although you may find some settings more comfortable than others, you should learn how to give and receive feedback in as many ways as possible. Then, when you are on the job and must respond to others' work, you will be prepared.

As a peer reader, then, you may be asked to play two roles: reader and evaluator. No matter which role you find yourself in, remember to collaborate with your writer. Try not to debate with the writer, weighing the value of your opposed positions, as if one of you could or should "win." If you work like this, you will compete to control the paper. The paper is the writer's, and it will remain so. T. S. Eliot praised Ezra Pound as a reader because "he didn't try to turn you into an imitation of himself. He tried to see what you were trying to do." React to what you read, and explain your reaction as accurately as possible. This kind of response can be simultaneously supportive of the writer and rigorous.

STRATEGIES FOR MAKING COMMENTS AS A PEER READER

Before you begin to comment on another student's writing, be sure that you have a clear sense of purpose. Are you going to summarize the writer's ideas? Are you going to apply specific criteria? Do you know what assignment the writer is responding to? What stage is the writer at? What have the writer and the teacher asked you to focus on? Take a minute or two to picture yourself in your role as a reader. Remind yourself that this is not your paper, but someone else's work and that you must respond to it, not rewrite it. You need to be sure that you read what the writer has written, not what may be in your head. This step may seem superfluous, but without a clear sense of purpose, your comments will be muddy and scattered. Just as with any other kind of writing, you need to know who you are and who you are addressing.

Once you have a clear sense of your purpose, you are ready to read the paper, looking first at what it says and later at how it says it. As you read, you will undoubtedly begin to notice strengths and weaknesses, and you may feel the urge to make comments even before you have finished reading the piece once. Try to resist this urge. If you feel that you must take notes because you might lose your train of thought, make them on a separate piece of paper. Often the questions and problems that you have in reading the first part of the paper will be redefined or answered in the latter part. Get a picture of the whole paper before you make comments on it. This strategy will also prevent you from dwelling on one aspect of the paper.

After you have read the paper, take a separate sheet and make some notes about the paper's main idea and structure. If you have been given a list of questions to answer, sketch out some responses to those questions. If you must respond to the paper without guiding questions, sort your responses into descriptions of what you've read, points that interested you and/or that might be expanded, places where you were confused, and any gross grammatical or mechanical problems that impaired your reading. Glance over your comments. If you respond to every feature of the writer's text, the writer won't know where to begin revising it. The author will simply stare at the sea of ink and wonder which problems interfered most with your comprehension and enjoyment of the material. Remember that a writer cannot attend to too many different responses at once, and so sort your reactions, determining which of your comments are most important. What information would most help the writer at this point? Are there a number of related comments that you could combine? For example, if a writer assumes that her audience requires very formal writing, this may lead her to use inflated words and to write redundantly or circuitously. If a writer's argument is not strong, her organization and word choice will probably be weak as well. If you find related comments, try to address yourself to the "root" concern — audience, soundness of argument, or whatever. Always remember to address large essay-level concerns before sentence-level responses. Even if the writer's style is nearly impenetrable, it may clear up when the writer has a better sense of her content and audience. The point is that you should neither dwell on one concern exclusively nor provide so many comments that the writer just gets confused.

Whether you are discussing a text that you have written or one that you have read, it is very important that you address the writing and not the writer. Writing is a very intimate act; it exposes us. Try not to say, "You're wrong," but rather point to statements in the text that seem invalid. If both writer and reader know the importance of addressing the text, then either of you can speak up if you feel personally attacked during the revising process.

Whether answering questions on a form or responding directly on the paper, a good peer reader is always specific. Nothing is more frustrating for a writer than having someone tell her that her writing is unclear, but not where. And the vague "I liked this paper" comment can be more frustrating and upsetting than a rigorous critique. If you do not give the writer specifics, it will seem as if you either read the paper quickly or don't care about it. Check your responses to see if every generalization that you make is supported by an example of why you were surprised, angered, or delighted.

Another excellent way to provide specifics is to explain why you reacted as you did. If you write, "This seems to contradict para 1 on p 4," say why. "Here you say that Huck Finn is a racist, but on page 4 (para 1) you called him 'tolerant.' I'm confused. Contradiction?" If you say that you find a sentence awkward, say why. If a point seems irrelevant, say why. Remember that the writer certainly did not set out to contradict herself, write awkwardly, or include irrelevancies. Simply telling her that her prose has these problems may not help her understand *how* her prose has misled or confused you. Instead of saying, "I disagree with you," be more specific about how you disagree. You might say, for example, "I disagree with your definition of religion — it doesn't seem like addiction to me." Comments like this give writers a more concrete sense of the audience they are addressing. Often I find that students are good at giving specific negative comments to each other, but that their positive comments remain very general. The same reader who will respond, "This sentence makes no sense after the previous one because you've changed the subject" might say, "I like this introduction" without saying what pleased him about the introduction. It is just as important to explain why and how a paper succeeds as to point out why and how it needs work.

As you read your classmate's paper, it will be quite natural for you to call on your skills as a writer and begin to see how the paper might be rewritten. But if you begin to revise the work in your head, you may well impose your own agenda on the writer's paper. In any case, you should not rewrite the paper. React to the work, but let the writer make the decisions that are necessary to revise it. Telling the writer "Move this para to p.4" is not helpful. Why do you think that the paragraph needs to be moved? Try using questions to point out specific problems in the essay without determining or directing the writer's revision. Reacting with "I'm lost. How does this paragraph relate to the one before it?'' is clear and detailed, but leaves the writer free to respond as she likes.

Although you do not want to rewrite the paper you are commenting on, you may want to discuss or propose strategies for the writer to follow in revising. In other words, readers and writers can exchange ''tips'' on revising strategies. If you recognize that the paper you are reading needs to be reorganized, share with the writer the tasks you would undertake to revise the paper. Don't tell her to put page 4 before page 2, but rather suggest that she cut the paper into chunks and reshuffle those chunks, or that she outline her draft to check its structure.

Concentrating on the tasks that lie ahead for the writer keeps your tone positive and upbeat. The most important quality in a peer reader may well be empathy, the ability to adopt someone else's point of view temporarily and to help her develop it. By focusing on ways in which the writer can respond, your comments can be supportive without losing their usefulness and rigor. They focus both you and the writer on the future, not on the past, and they allow you to be direct and honest without being mean or combative.

When you work hard to see the world through the writer's eyes and give her detailed, focused feedback, it is sometimes very difficult to watch her reject your suggestions or find other ways of reworking her paper. Once you have empathized with the reader, you may expect her to empathize with you. You must remind yourself, however, that the writer does not ''work for'' you. She is writing her own paper, and your comments will be extremely valuable to her, whether she reworks the paper exactly as you expected or not. Do not discount your contribution to the paper, even if you see little evidence of it in the final draft. Your comments will be in the writer's mind as she reworks the paper — even if she wants to ignore them, she won't be able to.

Exercise on Designing Questions for a Peer Reader.   In a group, make a list of ten questions that readers might address in responding to an upcoming paper assignment in this class. Be sure that the list contains about equal numbers of questions that ask the peer reader to respond as a reader and those that position the reader as a judge. When you hand these in to the teacher, she can select from among these questions as she designs a reader response form for that assignment.

Exercise on Being a Peer Reader.   Read the following paper (with its peer reader's comments) and discuss them. Has this peer reader done a good job? How could this reader improve her work? Revise the comments in order to improve them. You may choose to add comments, delete comments, expand responses, revise suggestions, or reword statements. Be prepared to submit your revised set of comments to the teacher.

Negligence and Inadvertence *You may want to name the article*

We would assume his paper would give his point of view, you can skip this and move right into mentioning what his view is.

While dealing with the issue of criminal responsibility, H. L. A. Hart comments on Dr. Turner's arguments and gives his (point of view.) This paper will consider the section entitled, "Negligence and Inadvertence" and present its relevance to both moral and legal responsibility.

This is repetitive.

The crux of Hart's argument is centered around the definition of negligence as, "a *word choice?* state of mind." This seems a bit (harsh.) *How is the definition harsh?*

Rather then claim negligence as a state of *(this should be "implying"* mind, infering something that cannot be controlled, I see it as more of a conscious decision to disregard some precaution. *Whats?* Regardless, Hart describes (it's) validity concerning criminal responsibility with reference to manslaughter. First of all he works under the condition that someone can

Are you saying that negligence is separate from intention and either one can cause responsibility?

be held criminally responsible only if he *isn't this repeating the same thing?* had it in his mind or had an intention to cause bodily harm. This holds well, for how can someone be held responsible for someone's death if the action that caused it was involuntary? Only when the action was caused by negligence.

So a dilemma is presented: if one is

criminally responsible only if bodily harm was intended, then it should follow that one *of* is not criminally responsible if bodily harm was not intended. But this can be easily disproved. Hart uses the example of a construction worker mending a roof in a busy part of town and the debris of his work [is] thrown down. *How can you construct this around an active verb?* It is quite obvious that the worker's only intention is to complete his job in a clear area; nevertheless, if someone is walking by and is hurt by the falling material, the worker must be held responsible for the injury. Why? Because he was negligent--he failed to take any precautionary measures or even consider the consequences of material falling into a street.

clear statement of relation between negligence and responsibility!

Just as the worker is held criminally responsible for the consequences, he is similarly held morally responsible. Although Hart does not discuss moral implications regarding negligence, I have come to the conclusion that moral responsibility must be ascribed to one who has been negligent, even if he/she is not found criminally responsible. But this circumstance is rare, for if one is found to be criminally responsible, it is assumed that a contributing factor to this verdict is the person's failure to be morally responsible in the given situation.

awk style revise

Why? Can you back up your asser

While pondering the issue of moral

responsibility and it's relation to

I don't see how this example explores the possibility of criminal resp. without moral responsibility

criminal responsibility, I became

This sounds like you want to be criminally resp.!

intruiged with the concept of being criminally responsible without being morally responsible. What if a robber came into a bank with the sole intent of making off with the money, and he went even so far as to bring a toy gun so that no one would be hurt? Should he be held both criminally and

Such as? Do you mean outcomes other than depriving the bank of money?

morally responsible for any unfavorable outcome even though he went out of his way to insure that no one would be caused any bodily harm? The answer is *Why?* yes, and implies that even under good intentions, he is held accountable for both breaking the law and causing harm.

Can you make a smoother transition?

Then there is the question of the degree of negligence required tomake a person accountable ornot. Dr. Turner asserts that a concept of degrees of negligence is absurd but both *Hart and I* myself and Hart disagree with such an assertion. If we return to the example of the construction worker and examine the situation, we find there are certain levels of precautions he could have taken that would have deterred anyone from being injured. They range from the obvious (looking before throwing down debris) to the less obvious (shouting down to any pedestrians to beware, or putting up a warning sign). The less obvious the precaution is, the more thought and care was *"must be"* exerted in the task. Therefore, the more

Starting this sentence with the adjective Blameworthy *followed by a "to be" verb causes your sentence to get bogged down in awkward prepositional phrases. What is the subject / verb connection in this sentence? Can you build the sentence around it?*

obvious the precaution, the more he is

responsible ⟨ ⟩ and blameworthy. *unnecessary*

Blameworthy is a term that designates a definite tone concerning the responsibility of the person in question. Hart relates negligence with *"to"* blameworthiness only to enforce and introduce another concept to negligence, that of inadvertence.

While the dictionary defines inadvertence as, ''unintentional, accidental,'' Hart prefers to describe it as a direct translation of negligence. I strongly disagree because while negligence connotes blame or reproach, inadvertence implies blamelessness. *Why?* Yet, both terms are connected by the fact that A) harm is caused to someone or something and B) both could *So how / the ter* have been prevented. *diff*

And prevention, or the amount of mental exertion needed to ensure that no one is *can prevention itself be the base?* harmed, is the base for a decision of criminal or moral responsibility.

You start the paragraph discussing prevention and then move into something else.

Returning to the issue of manslaughter, Hart feels that two questions should be asked in order to determine one's responsibility. The first is if harm was intended, and the second is if he acted in ''a fit of inadvertence.'' But then he has contradicted himself because he previously

mentioned that for criminal
responsibility, mere inadvertence is not
enough. Therefore he resorts to the claim
that an act of negligence is essentially the
same as acting in a fit of inadvertence.

If for criminal responsibility
negligence and inadvertence are alike, does
the same hold for moral responsibility? If
someone was harmed during the robbery where
the robber had come only with a toy gun, the
harm could not be attributed to negligence.
The harm was not premeditated, nor was it
caused by a failure to take normal
precautions. It was caused by a distraction
from the main event - - it was caused
inadvertently. Therefore, unlike

what does this mean?

negligence alone, whose implications
follow both criminal and moral
responsibility, negligence and
inadvertence work together criminally but
not morally.

Do you mean that criminal law considers negligence and inadvertence to be identical but they can be separated when making moral judgments?

There is one final point concerning
negligence that Hart encounters. It deals
with the act of ommission It is ⨯ his
opinion that negligence (being a state of
mind) is the ommission of precautions that
are required by a certain standard.
Ommission in itself is a heavily discussed
concept with regard to criminal and moral
responsibility. Usually one is convicted
due to actions that are committed, but but,

Again, how does the sp. point flow from what has gone before? Transition?

in a sense, the ommission of an action is committing an action, just as not deciding between two choices is a decision in itself. But I regard his reference to ommission as too harsh. Instead of an ommission of precautions, I see it as more of a failure to take necessary precautions.

Aren't those the same?

In conclusion, I agree with some general areas of Hart's arguments, but find the definitons of some terms inaccurate. The question of criminal responsibility is solved but moral responsibility is left up to the reader. It is this question of morality which will help the reader relate these theories to the "real world," giving a more universal perspective to such a narrow concept.

Kim

You seem to have a good sense of organization because your paper begins with a clear progression of ideas from paragraph to paragraph. However, toward the middle of your paper you start neglecting transitions and losing paragraph focus. See if you can state the main purpose of each paragraph and see if material in that para. all relates to the focus. Also be careful of making assertions and then failing to develop your reasons behind them.

On the sentence level, you need to work on precision. Be aware of repetitive constructions ("the crux is centered around") choice of vague words (how can a definition be "harsh"?), and passive constructions. If these cloud your prose, it is hard for the reader to see your message.

If you have questions about my further suggestions, just give me a call!

—Beth (343-4783)

Exercise on Peer Response to Specific Question.   As an individual,
read this student paper and comment on it in response to the questions
that follow it. In your group, compare responses. Where does the group
agree and disagree about the paper? If there is disagreement, what
causes it? Is it the result of the text or the personal backgrounds of the
readers? Then individually, write a one-page reflection on your work as
a peer reader. How did you proceed? What did you like about your
responses? What might you change in the future? Submit your response
sheet and your reflections to your teacher.

The assignment for this paper was to take notes on five pieces of art
at a local museum and then to write a paper connecting three of them in
any way.

When I was a child, my father was red. It was not
because he was an American Indian, or had high blood
pressure, or even sunburn; to me he just appeared red.
When I drew pictures of my father in art class it was a big
red crayola with which I made the outlines of his head.
His lips were black and wide and he had no hair whatsoever
and a stiff, boxed brown shirt with a blue tie. This upset
my teacher, Miss Inkblatt. ''Alan L.,'' she would say,
discerning me from Alan P., ''use the peach for skin, not
the red.'' Not even a peach is the color of peach was my
silent retort. Peach crayons looked like Band-Aids. I
assumed that the heads of the parents of my classmates
looked like little round Band-Aids with eyes. However,
my father could not be drawn into only two dimensions. He
had width and heighth as wax on paper, but then there was
much more. My father was a wicked tyrant with a firey red
head and flaming orange ears. He dominated my life and
injected it with fear. His face was not grey-beige like a
Band-Aid, but bright red.

As I saw my father day to day, he was all my fears
personified. His image was affected by my emotional
relationship to it. To sketch upon paper my mental image,
then, meant not a round beige circle but a hotly-colored
monster. There is this essential quality in all that we
call art; it is the transformation of real perceptions
into ones affected by the individual. Examples of this
quality, it being essential, should be readily available.
In fact, they are the basis for every piece in every

museum. At the Museum of the Rhode Island School of Design in Providence, Rhode Island, are three paintings which, although widely separated by time and by the skill of their creators, all use their subjects, and especially trees, in a similar manner. The earliest of these pieces was painted in 1871 by Claude Monet and is titled "Hyde Park, London." It depicts the park in early Spring. Several broad and tidy rolling hills in the foreground lead the eye back towards a washed skyline of the city, whose grey, geometrical, static buildings are without sharp detail. The sky above the city is softly blue. In the park itself, there are walking paths criss-crossing the area and several rigid Victorian couples with top hats and parasols ceremoniously promenading about. There are three trees: one on the left center of the canvas; another, diminished in size, behind the first; and one to the right of center, perched on the primary hill of the foreground. The trees are grey, with highlights of brown, but are nondescript. They have solid boles poked insecurely into the already unconvincing earth, and the limbs often fail to meet one another at the joints. They seem to involuntarily poke out at the sky, like the bristles on a whale-wisker clothes brush.

The trees reflect well subject. The entire false-feeling and uninterested landscape, with its trees who looked bored by the hazy sun and grow nothing but translucent leaves, is a sustaining theme parallel to that of the cold and pre-programmed persons who saunter through the springtime park. If one may conject over centuries and continents, the work is Monet the Impressionist's reaction to the scene. In unhumanized reality the trees are green, the buildings distinct, and the people are frolicking. However, Monet was a man and an artist. His rendition of Hyde Park revealed his personal transformation of objective perception into subjective.

George Bellows created a similar canvas in the 1920's called "Rain on the River." In it, a strong diagonal is formed from top left to lower right by a somber, lead-hued river. Above the river is a city scape, like that of Manhattan. As in the Monet, the looming city is foreboding and rejectful. Covering two thirds of the canvas, below the river, is a park with barren trees and paths lined by street lights. Rain falls violently upon the river and its surroundings. Two tall and slender, limbless trees set upon the park a feeling of harsh vacancy with their own stark diagonal which imperfectly parallels that of the river. Blues, greys, browns, and sienna comprise the scheme of color. The trees in the park enforce a strong disconnection with the more desirable view. There is submission to more powerful natural forces and a sense of loneliness for want of a single person in a space expecting people. An unhumaness struck the artist.

It would be a mistake to think that either artist intended that his work be interpreted as I have done. The parks were before them as they painted, and their parks are before me as I transform them again and offer the results. Correct interpretation is not at issue here. The interpretation is of importance to individuals only. It is to the universe of creative expression that this paper hopes to lend understanding. That something is at all a work of true art is not a bounded question; that the need for active skill rests with the artist rather than with the viewer is so. That Monet and Bellows saw trees and successfully transformed them from pure perceptions into felt entities implies artistic creation.

The last work to be dealt with is entitled "State House," and was painted in 1980, in Providence, by a Portuguese immigrant named George Araujo. This painter is untrained compared to the two previous, but, although primitive, his works reflect with amazing similarity the attributes of Monet and Bellows. The trees of Araujo are less refined in their presentation. George Araujo only recently began painting seriously and has never attended an art school. Thus, in "State House" his trees haphazardly surround the building which rests on its hill in the area above left center. The trees have few limbs and appear intent on guarding the law and its makers in the state house with their feeble, leafless arms araised. The effect is to leave the building lonely and tyranical in its rule of the composition. The trees spread out from it like rotted roots from a once more majestic trunk. But, that such meaning can be extracted rests on the also being a group of green, fully leaved trees in a small foreground corner beneath the state house. When viewing the painting, the greenery there admits a renascent energy that transcends the feeling of inevitable decay.

Araujo is significant because he is primitive and untrained. Still the artist performs his task; his impression is conveyed, or rather is there for others to be impressed by. He does not simply represent trees with paint. He represents himself with trees.

It is possible that the young Monet, Bellows and Araujo were entreated to realize their own fathers as two-dimensional Band-Aids also. In denying the restriction, however, they succeeded in drawing from humanized visions for their subjects. This is the essential quality of their art. A man is grey-beige; my father is red.

READER RESPONSE QUESTIONS

1. Read the first paragraph and then pause. Write down what you expect the topic, purpose, and audience of the paper will be.
2. Now finish reading the paper. Were your expectations for the paper's topic, purpose, and audience fulfilled? If not, what do you now think the topic, purpose, and audience are?
3. What do you think the main idea or thesis of the paper is?
4. Summarize the paper, devoting one sentence to each paragraph.
5. What did you like best about the paper?
6. Did anything in the paper surprise you?
7. What two features of the paper most need improvement?

Exercise to "Exorcise the Ghost."   Read the following paper. First comment on it as a teacher might. Parody a teacher's comments. Then comment again as an inexperienced student peer reader might, also exaggerating your responses to the point of parody.

Topic: *How do advertisements shape modern values, attitudes, etc.?*

Advertisements of today do not shape modern values as much as advertising analists claim they do. From the standpoint of the viewer, I consider advertising of today to be designed only for the unstable, insecure and extremely gullable person as well as the uneducated child.

Only being one of these types of people, could I agree with advertising analysts.

How can any average, knowledgeable, basically secure individual be swayed, in establishing his or her values, by the advertisements of today? They merely insult human intellect by being set up for the IQ of a three or four year old. The developers design their advertisements for emotional appeal, popular appeal (the "in" things), and snob appeal. They are only failing when they do this because the average person sees right through the advertisement. That is, in consciously knowing what the developer is trying to accomplish in his advertisement he becomes unmoved by the purpose of it.

If a person were unstable, insecure and very gullable advertisements could play an important part on the origin of their values. Because he is unstable, emotional advertisement appeal could move him in decisions. Being insecure would influence his attitude toward advertisements of popular and snob appeal. Also if he is gullable enough to not see through them he could easily be influenced by them.

Children of little formal education are probably most influenced by advertising. Saturday morning television is filled with advertising for children. Obviously the exciting new toys that "Tommy" or "Susi" have are ideally what the child wants. At that age he is striving to be accepted by as many other youngsters as possible. By having those toys He is now more like them. Also he has the attitude that "Tommy's" parents got him this toy can I have it too? " Advertisements make the child expect these things otherwise he may psychologically think his parents don't care about his wants. He may even think they don't love him as much as "Tommy's" parents because of the great emphasis placed on having these toys through advertising.

Values and attitudes of today are shaped mostly by individual or group experiences among piers, family and friends of the opposite sex. Actual everyday occurances, contacts, and conversation mold the values of persons today. These person to person relationships have much more of a dynamic influence on ones attitudes, values etc. Because of close ties among certain individuals, there is more influential contact also. This type of value and

attitude shaping is also one the intellectual level of
that specific individual or group of individuals.

Exercise on Responding to Successful Prose.   Here is a fairly successful student paper. But we know that all writers can revise. Write a
prose paragraph in response to this paper (a note to the author), suggesting ways in which the piece might be improved. In a group, compare your paragraphs. How did you agree? Disagree? Why?

Alcohol is a generalized central nervous system
depressant. As such, its effect is to depress the centers
of the brain that mediate inhibitions, judgement, and
control. Individual neurons become less excitable,
repolarize more slowly after excitation, and exhibit
reduced spontaneous electrical activity. Synaptic nerve
transmission is impaired. Spinal reflexes are depressed.
In addition, neuromuscular coordination (speech, gait,
manual dexterity) is reduced, as is visual acuity, and
perception of pain and fatigue. Why then, does a little
drinking so often seem to have a stimulating effect?

In the past, alcohol had been thought of as a
uniformly depressant drug. Excited speech and behavior
occurring after a little drinking had been attributed to
the aforementioned depressant effects of alcohol on the
mechanisms that normally regulate these activities.
Although this may be true, this was widely accepted as the
total explanation. It is now recognized that alcohol,
ultimately a depressant, does indeed first act as a
stimulant.

The first action of alcohol on neural tissue is to
irritate, agitate, or stimulate. Although spinal reflexes
become depressed as intoxication increases, they are
initially enhanced. Responses to the irritant effect of
alcohol can be observed in the gastrointestinal tract.
The nausea that can occur after the use of alcohol probably
stems from gastrointestinal inflammation. Diarrhea may
be provoked by the irritant properties of various oils
present in most alcoholic beverages.

The concept of alcohol as a stimulant has been
further demonstrated in an experiment where intelligent

subjects were given small doses of alcohol (2 – 4 ounces whiskey). They were required to solve highly demanding intellectual problems such as Boolean logic. It was found that their performance after ingesting a small amount of whiskey was superior to their performance when sober or following the ingestion of larger amounts of whiskey.

Finally, there may be more mundane reasons for the apparent stimulation observed after a little drinking. The calories from the alcohol provide a ''quick energy boost.'' In social situations someone may just feel ''high'' or happy the minute a drink is in their hand. It may be a signal that it is time to party. There would be an initial stimulation until the depressant effects set in. So, alcohol can be seen initially as a stimulant having both physiological and psychological manifestations. Yet the ultimate effect of alcohol in high doses is always as a depresant. The euphoria and excitement that one derives from drinking, with increased intoxication, lead to confusion, stupor, coma, and perhaps death.

Exercise on Commenting at Different Stages of the Writing Process.

Read the following student paper. In a three-person group, assign one person to respond as if this were an early draft, another as if it were written midway through the process, and a third as if the writer considered the paper almost finished. As you comment on the paper individually, try to find related concerns in it and address root problems that may be generating a number of surface errors. Then, back in your group, look to see how the stage of writing determined the focus of your comments. Did you find different underlying errors if you assumed that the paper was at different stages in its development? Be prepared to share your conclusions with the class as a whole.

There is extensive literature on the phenomena of racism and prejudice. Many writers have dug deep down into the annals of history to find the origins, causes and effects of such phenomena. Both William Maltby in his <u>The Black Legend in England</u> and Philip Wayne Powell in his <u>Tree of Hate</u> offer splendid and vivid accounts of the origins and nature of the overwhelming resentment and hatred directed at the Spaniards. These books are basically reflective of a host of writers who have analyzed the origins and effects of racism and prejudice in a microcosmic way, in Maltby's and Powell's case it was an analysis of "The Black Legend", and yet have failed to offer both solutions to these phenomena as well as forecast these solutions in a macrocosmic way. In this paper, I will bravely offer a potential solution to these universal phenomena, racism and prejudice which plague all of mankind.

Living in a world that is festering with hatred and prejudice, I find it not only interesting but also pertinent to reach for some type of panacea that will help alleviate these growing problems. In this paper I wish to define racism as a "racial prejudice or discrimination" and prejudice as "an irrational attitude of hostility directed against an individual, a group, a race or their supposed characteristics." What should be clear is that both phenomena are based on preconceived judgements and opinions. As stated before, many writers have done fabulous jobs in discovering the roots of these preconceived judgements, but very few writers have offered solutions to these touchy issues. These feelings of prejudice and racism are omnipresent in modern day society. As Professor Padden explained, "anything that tends to be unacceptable is noted." Professor Padden was referring to the Englishman's first encounter with the Negro. Since the Negro was obviously different from the Englishman, the Englishman immediately formed biased judgements and opinions of the Negro.

In today's society, which is characterized by sky-high crime rates, distrust of one's neighbors and a general aloofness on the part of most everyone who walks the streets, one probably feels that there is no hope in restoring harmony to society and in creating a world in which deep seated prejudices are eliminated. There is though a potential solution to the phenomena of racism and prejudice and that is the simple concept of reciprosity. If each and every individual would do unto others as he or she would expect others to do unto himself or herself, then basically hate, prejudice and racism would be abolished. I feel very strongly that if the concept of reciprosity were properly implemented upon mankind then we would no longer need guns, armys and wars to solve our problems. It may be difficult to grasp the significance of this concept, but I feel once one understands how it is to be implemented then he or she will appreciate the magnitude of the reciprosity element. First and foremost, we must begin the implementation process in the United States, for not only is this our motherland but being a world power the United States has a great deal of influence on other countries--therefore other countries might follow the United States as an example. In implementing the concept of reciprosity two very important stages must be presented.

Since a majority of resentment and prejudice, especially in the United States, stems from economic insecurity, we must first solve our economic inadequacies. Though, this is a monumental and taxing task, as evidenced by the Bush Administration's difficulty in trying to balance the budget, it is not impossible to achieve. Through the proper economic policies and advice of competent economic experts we can and we will be able to say someday that everyone in our country is economically secure. Once individuals are economically secure, that is they are sufficiently able to provide for food, clothing, shelter and education without having to steal, bribe or use any illegal means in order to achieve their ends, then we are moving in the right direction. Since economic security is no longer a problem, then crime will thus subside. As economic security becomes a persistent pattern of security for Americans, then in time jealousies, resentment and prejudices will slowly become eradicated. This assertion is based on the assumption that if people are financially secure, then they will not feel resentful or jealous of the individual who was always financially secure--thus eliminating many of the hostilities and prejudices that were present. By creating a sense of economic security with the American people, we have moved one step closer to our prospective goal. The next stage, that of creating an overall feeling of reciprosity is more difficult to implement.

In order to establish a widespread feeling of reciprosity among the American people, we must start with our youth, for they are our future generation. We must establish specific centers or mini-societies in which there exists no outside biases or prejudices, so that these children will be "brainwashed" so to speak with the notion of reciprosity. It is important to note that only the newborn can be placed in these special centers, for even young children have prejudices and biases as reflected by their environment, friends and parents. These special centers should not be associated with science-fiction futuristic societies in which everyone resembles Dr. Spock on "Star Treck." These mini-societies are more like special universities in which our youth are taught from day one to do unto his or her peers as they would do unto himself or herself. Once this concept of reciprosity has been firmly entrenched into the minds of our future generation, we will have succeeded in creating a group of individuals who no longer live with prejudiced or racist notions. The concept of reciprosity is not an erudite thought, but the implementation process may seem to be somewhat futuristic.

RESPONDING TO A READER'S COMMENTS

In peer review, it sometimes seems as if the reader is in control, making comments, prioritizing responses, and suggesting strategies for the writer. But, in fact, the writer controls the entire procedure by preparing a text for the reader, directing the reader's attention, and leading any oral discussions of his work. And it is especially important for you, the writer, to be in control as you revise in response to readers' comments.

If you read your paper aloud and receive oral feedback from a group, you may well begin to think you've lost control. You will want to direct the discussion, but it is hard to define questions, record several readers' reactions, worry about time constraints, and feel in control of your own ideas — all at the same time. For this reason, if you receive oral feedback from a large group, you may want to appoint a group coordinator to help you. While you set the agenda for the conversation, the coordinator assures that all readers are heard, that no one becomes defensive, that circular arguments don't waste the group's time, and that no one dominates the discussion or uselessly repeats points. The coordinator is a bit like a mediator, keeping the conversation moving, and involving all parties. You will want to consider having a coordinator in your group if the group is quite large (more than four), if the readers have not had time to prepare their responses, or if the topic of the paper is highly controversial or emotional.

Whether you read or listen to reaction to your paper, try to remain open. Suspend judgment and resist the all-too-human urge to be defensive. You may find that you want to say, "But I did that just two sentences later. . . ." If you need to clear up a misunderstanding so that you and your reader can communicate, then do so. Otherwise, listen and try to understand what the reader has to say. Peter Elbow reminds writers:

> When people start to argue, you know something is wrong because there is nothing to argue about. There is no right answer to defend, no wrong answer to defeat. The only goal is to learn what happened in each reader. Afterward the writer may want to decide for herself which of two conflicting reactions is most likely to occur in her target audience, but right now her job is to learn those reactions and if possible even to experience them. Arguments will interfere with her doing so.

In other words, you need to adopt the same stance toward your readers that they took toward your paper — be empathetic. If you are trying to defend yourself or even just to sort and judge your reader's comments, you will not be able to hear them fully. Listen first; sort and evaluate later.

This does not mean, however, that you and your readers should not talk through your disagreements. If two readers disagree, or if you as the writer strongly disagree with your readers, pursue that disagreement. In discussing different reactions, remember that you are not searching to determine which one is right and which wrong, but rather to see what this disagreement can illuminate. What can it tell you about your text? Because this is your goal, you may decide to stop discussing the varied readers' reactions and move on to a new topic before all the differences are resolved. You will eventually resolve the differences as you weigh alternatives and revise. Don't try to make decisions about how to revise while readers are still providing you with information.

As you read written comments, you may want to take notes, recording your questions or ideas for revision. If your readers are giving you oral comments, you will want to keep a different kind of record. Most important, you will need to keep track of what you're told. This is the only written record that you will have to refer to later when you are revising all by yourself. Try to keep as full and accurate a record as possible. Few people can write fast enough to record their readers' responses and their own thoughts at once. But if you can, write down your own thoughts on a separate piece of paper or in a separate column. At the end of the revising session, when your readers have voiced their reactions and answered your questions, be sure to thank them for their time.

Once you have read or listened to the reactions to your paper, you will want to revise. If you can allow yourself a break, however, take one. Whether you received responses from one reader or several, you will want to let those remarks sink in before you act on them. Get some distance from the details of your readers' responses. You may find that your subconscious will begin to sort through the comments for you, retaining the ones you found useful and forgetting others. Since you have a record of the readers' responses, you don't need to worry about losing track of them.

As you sit down to your paper, you will want to re-establish your own sense of it. You may not have looked at the piece in a couple of days. First reread the draft, taking notes about revisions you would like to make. Then, after you've thought about the changes that you feel are warranted, consult your readers' responses, accepting useful suggestions and rejecting useful ones. Remain open to your readers' comments, but remember that this is your paper — your name is the one that will appear on the final draft. You do not need to respond to every suggestion that you get, but you should consider them all. Sometimes you will find that readers are reacting to the same problem but in different words. A reader may urge you to expand a particularly successful part of the paper, but that section may become irrelevant as you revise. Keep control of the paper. Your readers' reactions are data that you will interpret. But you will need to find your own solutions to the problems posed by your text. After you have made revisions, give yourself a break and then reread the work to be sure that all the parts fit together smoothly. Finally, you will want to run the paper through a spell checker, if you have one.

Of course, the process of peer review can be recursive. You can try your ideas out on a friend early in the process, do some writing, get reactions from readers, revise based on their reactions, and still want another reader to look at the piece. Don't be afraid to seek additional response. But don't let yourself get confused by too many responses. Especially in the later stages of writing, you may well ask that readers look at only one or two features of the paper.

The important things to remember are that you are in control and that your writing is not hopeless. Sometimes in the middle of revision, it is very easy to get discouraged. If this happens, take a break. Look again at the satisfying parts of your paper. Learn to trust yourself as a reviser and keep going. Sometimes asking a reader to respond to your work by describing what he likes best can help, but learning to trust yourself is also a very valuable skill.

Getting the most from peer review, then, requires a paradoxical combination of retaining authority over your paper and remaining open to others' reactions. You must listen and learn, but not be too easily swayed. You must have a commitment to your work, but still be willing to alter it. You must trust your abilities, but know you can improve. Keeping a diary of your reactions to peer review may help you chart your progress as you define your role as a writer.

CONCLUDING REMARKS

Peer review may be the most important skill that you learn in this class. It is a skill that you can use in the future, no matter what profession you choose. When it works well, it can establish a supportive environment in which to work and learn. One student, describing her experience with peer review in a studio art class, explained that although she was hesitant at first, scared that her work might be severely criticized, she found the class rewarding.

If you've gone along since the beginning with the same people it never comes across as this awful criticism. It's very supportive. You have to stand there and face something for four hours and know that you didn't solve anything. You're emotionally drained when you're finished. Then, the next day, people help you decide why or say, "No, I think it came out all right; don't be so upset," or "This is fantastic." You just keep picking each other up out of the pits and saying, "You've done something good here," or "Why don't you try this?" [The teacher] is more or less a conductor. He shouldn't dominate it. It's never just a grade scrawled across the top; it's a suggestion.

Knowing how to seek others' criticism and learn from their expertise without belittling your own convictions is very valuable. But don't let peer revision stop you from writing. As Peter Elbow warns us:

It's easy to know when you should start getting feedback. Just keep in mind what's more important than what: writing is more important than sharing your writing with readers; and sharing your writing with readers is more important than getting feedback from them. That is, if sharing begins to stop you from writing, then don't share. And if getting feedback begins to stop you from writing or sharing, then stop getting feedback. Writing is what's most important. But when you can share and get feedback *without* hampering your writing, then you will benefit enormously from those two activities.

Every time you revise or comment on someone else's work, you learn new strategies and discover new concerns. No two revision sessions are exactly the same. Writing and revising are sort of like building and breaking off a relationship. Each time we leave a relationship, we think that we have learned from it. "I'll know how to handle myself next time," we think. But the next time we encounter new problems. We find new joys. Keeping a diary or log of these discoveries can help you work through relationships and through revising. You might set aside a notebook just for jotting down tricks that you discover to make writing and revising easier. Then, when you are stuck next time, you can read over your list of strategies — things to do and things to avoid. You can benefit from your own experience.

Exercise on Giving and Receiving Peer Feedback.   Your teacher will give you a paper assignment to draft individually. After your draft is ready for peer review, write three general questions that might be part of a reader response sheet for this assignment. In a group of three, compile your questions into a reader response form. Write out your form and copy it for each group member. Then, at the end of the form that is to accompany your paper, tell the reader what you would do if you had 24 more hours to work on the paper and add three questions specific to your essay. Exchange papers and complete peer response sheets for each other.

After you have returned the papers and the response sheets to the writers, discuss the papers as a group. Allow writers to clarify or challenge readers' responses. Following this group session, take some notes about it. Did you notice any patterns in the group? Did individuals respond differently? Can you make any hypotheses about the effects of gender or ethnicity or perceived success in school on peer response?

Revise your paper, based on the readers' responses and your sense of what needs doing. Before submitting it to the teacher, reflect on your reaction to this process, concluding by naming yourself in the mythic style — for example, She Who Wears a Hair Shirt or He Who Puts Cotton in His Ears. This name should appear somewhere on your final paper.

Exercise on Defining Reader-Writer Relationships.   In a group of three to five, discuss how the relationship between reader and writer is and is not like other mutually responsible partnerships. You might contrast it to the parent-child relationship or the situation of shipwrecked people in a lifeboat. Decide which of your comparisons might yield the best analogy and write a paragraph explaining that analogy. Be honest — don't be extremely cheery just to please the teacher or cynical just to get a laugh. Be prepared to read your group's analogy to the class.

Exercise on Conferencing Techniques.   Exchange papers in simple pairs. After you have read each other's essays, prepare for a conference between writer and reader. This will be a coached conference, however, and so two pairs will be working together in a group totaling four students. One pair should begin to discuss one of their two papers, watched closely by the other pair. Each member of the observing pair will take notes describing and analyzing the behavior of one of the conferring pair. After five minutes, the conference will pause and the observers will consult with the people they were watching, giving them feedback. Are they being defensive? Have they agreed about the basic content of the piece? Are they getting stuck on details? The conference will then proceed for another five minutes. Again, the observers will consult with the people they are coaching.

The conferring pair should discuss the second paper in the same way that they discussed the first. Again, the observers will consult with the conferring pair at five-minute intervals.

Finally, the two pairs should switch roles and repeat the exercise. Those who were the observers will now be the observed. (Adapted from Spear, 1988)

Exercise on Negotiating Peer Response and Teacher Evalua-tion.   As you participate in a peer review exercise, take notes before you give your paper to a reader. Consider what state your text is in. What is your main idea? What do you like about the paper now? What do you want to change? How close to being finished do you think it is? Exchange papers, respond, and return the papers to the writers. After you have heard your readers' responses (in writing and orally or in just one medium), take notes about what state you now think your text is in. Do you plan to work from the same main idea as you started with? What is the most useful contribution that a reader made to your understanding of your work? What do you think strengths of the essay are? What is your plan for revising it? After revising your work but before submitting it to the teacher, again take notes about what you like best and least about your final draft. What would you do if you had 24 more hours to work on the paper now?

When you get the paper back from the teacher, look carefully at his comments. Did he agree with your assessment of your work? Did he share your readers' reactions? Looking back over the notes that you took during the process of writing this paper, write a two-page discussion of how your paper evolved.

Summary Exercise.   In a group of about three students, study this chapter and complete the peer review sheet on pp. 59–61 for it. That is, looking at this chapter as if it were a paper describing revision and peer response, write an abstract of it, extend some of it, and doubt some of it. What additional advice should students have about peer revision? What advice here is inadequate? Then pick a section and revise it.

Variation.   Groups of students in the class review and revise different sections of the chapter. Then, when the revisions are assembled, the entire new chapter can be made available for everyone to read.

Suggested Paper Topics

1. Write a letter to the writers of a specific television sit-com, describing your reactions to their work. Point out the positive aspects of the show and offer suggestions for improvement. In other words, position yourself as a "peer viewer" and offer constructive criticism for the series. Assume that the writers are just about to start working on next season's shows.

2. Consider your last job or your last school and identify one major defect in it. Write a letter to your supervisor or your school's administration, describing this problem and offering one or more solutions. Be sure that you explain the principles that make your solutions preferable to the status quo.

3. Write an analytical description of yourself as a group member. What are your strengths? What do you need to improve?

4. Write a letter to me as the author of this book, responding to the suggestions and ideas in this chapter. What suggestions worked for you? What questions do you have? What suggestions would you have for revising the chapter?

5. Assume that you are on the editorial board for your college or town newspaper and that you have just been asked to comment on a recent editorial. Write a constructive response that will help the editor improve her work. You may agree or disagree with the content of the piece, but be sure to comment on the strengths and weaknesses of its presentation.

CHAPTER
4

WRITING A CO-AUTHORED PAPER OR REPORT

*C*hapter 3 discussed ways in which individual writers can work with the people around them as they create single-authored papers. Unquestionably, this is the most common kind of writing in college. But most professionals — doctors, lawyers, teachers, business executives, scientists, librarians — also write many documents in which they share authorship. The process of writing together is not all that different from the process of writing alone — it just takes more careful management and some psychological adjustment. After all, as I said in the first chapter, all writing is collaborative to some degree. We consult books and talk with friends as we write, even if we produce papers with only our name listed as the author. And the writing process — brainstorming, organizing ideas, drafting, and revising — does not change when you work with others. However, your relationship to your text and to those with whom you work does change. You are no longer the sole author of a text. People who write together frequently find it quite natural, but making the shift from writing alone in college to writing with others in the workplace can be difficult at first. The goal of this chapter is to prepare you to make that shift.

There are very few studies of collaborative writing, but recently Andrea Lunsford and Lisa Ede surveyed 1400 members of seven different professional organizations about the kinds of writing that they do. Ede and Lunsford then studied the collaborative writing projects that these professionals described. Much of this chapter is based on their work, reported in their book, *Singular Texts/Plural Authors*. This field is still relatively new, and you may discover important features of collaborative writing that I have not mentioned here. As you work through this chapter, you will be helping to break new ground in the teaching of writing.

DEFINING COLLABORATIVE WRITING

Although there are many ways in which people can collaborate on a text, we will focus here on papers that involve more than one person contributing directly to the creation of a text and so sharing responsibility for it. This usually means that a number of people interact directly at some point during the production of the text. Most often, a group brainstorms and plans a document that is researched and drafted by one or more individuals working alone. Then the draft is revised by the group and final stylistic editing is done by one person. In another common procedure, an individual may draft a text that is revised and published by a group. Collaborative writing involves shared production and/or responsibility for a text. In this way the group establishes the initial goals for the project and retains responsibility over the final text by revising it. Although one or more individual writers may actually draft the work, they are fulfilling the group's goals.

The issue of responsibility is very important here. When you are writing a paper on your own, you may consult with others as you plan your work and as you revise it, but you are always writing with your own goals in mind and you are always responsible for your own work. That is why you are the sole author listed on the title page. You get advice from others, but you can decide to accept or ignore that advice. Although you consult with others, you are the one who makes all the decisions about your own text. This is not true of collaborative writing. Although you may write a section of a group paper on your own, you will have to respect the group's intentions for the entire text.

Every kind of writing has been done collaboratively at some time, I suspect, from grocery lists to letters to multivolume history books. Although collaborative writing is not limited to any particular written form, it is used most often in long reports that involve large amounts of work or specialized knowledge. In order to produce the most complete and accurate text, writers with different areas of expertise collaborate to generate grant proposals, drafts of legislation, budgets, or technical reports. Consultants from different areas may work together to draft a business plan. Collaborative writing is also frequently used when a group wants to represent its feelings publicly. A political party's platform is written collaboratively because it must represent the group as a whole.

TYPES OF COLLABORATIVE WRITING

Although anything can be written collaboratively, there are three common kinds of collaborative texts. It is important to recognize these categories of collaborative writing because each defines authorship differently and assigns responsibility for the text to different people. If you are asked to be part of a writing team, you should know what kind of decision-making power you will have, what kind of writing you will need to do, and how your contribution to the project will be recognized. That way, you will not be surprised if you work very hard on a piece and find that you are not listed individually as an author for it. Nor will you be surprised by discovering that you are listed as an author of something that you simply edited.

Serial Writing

Serial writing involves a train of individuals working on a text. One person drafts the text, another receives and revises that text before passing it on to someone else for further revision, until the text at last reaches someone who approves it and signs it. This kind of document usually has only one visible author — the last person in the chain. In some cases, as the text passes along the chain, it is incorporated into larger and larger reports. In other cases, it remains a single text — a political candidate's brochure, for example. Another kind of serial writing involves one individual dictating a text to another, who transcribes and revises it. In this case, the first individual is usually the sole author. When a supervisor assigns a project to one of her employees, who then researches and drafts a document, which the supervisor revises and signs — that, too, is serial writing.

In serial writing, there is usually at least one hidden author. If a letter or report written by a series of people is questioned, the person signing the report will be officially held responsible for it. However, that individual may privately hold others underneath her responsible for problems in the text. In serial writing, the text is usually attributed to one person who is also officially responsible for it. For this reason, writers in a serial project often feel as if they're writing *for* someone rather than *with* them.

In serial writing, the authors rarely meet face to face. Instead, they communicate through the texts that they produce. Because only the last person will accept responsibility for the text, there is also no feedback loop — that is, the first author has little or no control over how his text is used or changed. The only exception to this is when supervisors assign work to their employees and then edit the same work. Here, however, those who draft a document still have little control over its final form. Authors in this situation rarely have a sense of group goals — they are relatively isolated individuals whose combined work produces a single-authored text. For this reason, serial writing is very much like writing alone, except for problems of coordination and communication.

Compiled Writing

Compiled writing also relies heavily on individual input, but each of the individuals retains some control over part of the final text and a reader can distinguish one person's contribution from another's. Common examples of compiled writing are a collection of essays addressing a common topic from a variety of perspectives, or a long technical report with sections that were obviously produced by individual writers. Unlike serial writing, compiled writing involves a strong sense of group authorship — the writers work toward a common goal. Yet they do not lose their individual identities as authors because some portion of the final text is directly attributable to each of them.

In some compiled writing projects, the group plans a project, then each member of the group writes a portion of the final document — an individual essay, a section of a longer report — and the group compiles and revises the entire work. Grant proposals are usually written this way. A legal advisor must write concerning the legal requirements of the grant, a fiscal advisor must address the budget, and a demographer must explain the survey techniques involved in evaluating it. Each writer works in the area of his expertise. Consultants' reports often follow this procedure. Sometimes collections of articles are written this way, too. If a group wants to publish their collected views on, say, the appropriateness of radical brain surgery like lobotomies, they might divide the task among individuals who would address the ethical ramifications, the success rate for various kinds of operations, and the financial cost of these procedures. Because the resulting essays will remain distinct, there is no need for them to conform to a single style, but the group might co-author an introduction for the collection.

In this kind of writing, the group may revise the final product or may even assign a single member of the group to act as editor. But because the group will take responsibility for the whole while individuals will take responsibility for sections of the text, any final editing must meet everyone's standards. Unlike serial writing, this kind of group writing involves many feedback loops. Compiled writing may occur when a supervisor assigns the writing of a document to an entire department, each member of the department writes her section of the document, and then the supervisor compiles and edits the final report. This is different from serial writing so long as the individuals who contribute to the final document are publicly acknowledged as the authors of their sections and so long as they therefore feel as if they are acting as part of a group. I am contributing to a compilation of articles now that involves individual authors passing their texts around to all the other contributing authors for feedback. Although we will retain individual authorship of our separate chapters, we benefit from each other's expertise and do not have to work so hard at imagining the reactions of various audiences to our points of view.

Compiled writing is commonly used for documents that require specialized knowledge or represent multiple perspectives. In either case, individuals need to work together toward a common goal, even though their individual contributions remain distinct.

Co-Authored Texts

In a co-authored text, it is very difficult (indeed, often impossible) to distinguish the work of one writer from another. A group of two or more people may be listed as the authors of a text, but the text reads like one written by a single author. The individuals have melded into a group. Look back at the statements in Chapter 2 about co-authoring (pp. 30–31). In some cases, individual authors become so subsumed in the group project that they are not even mentioned by name as the authors of a text. This kind of writing is sometimes simply attributed to a group like a corporation, a committee, or a laboratory. In the case of institutional authorship, some individuals who had no role in the writing of a document may be held accountable for it. For example, in the sciences, individuals who worked at a laboratory during the research of a given project may be listed as authors of the resulting report even if they have subsequently left the lab. In some cases, people have asked to be excluded from a list of authors because they did not agree with the way the final report or research turned out.

Co-authored writing is what most people would probably think of first if they were asked to describe collaborative writing. It is a large category encompassing books with two authors, articles with over 100 authors, corporate reports issued by an institution, committee reports, union contracts, and most laws, government reports, and group manifestos like the Declaration of Independence. Co-authored writing is most often used when the final product reflects the sentiments of the group as a whole. The multiple perspectives that are preserved in compiled writing are not important here. Because of the need to agree on the substance and form of the document, this kind of writing is quite time consuming. But it is the only way to bring many perspectives into alignment, if a large number of people must "sign off" on a document.

There are many different procedures for producing a co-authored work. They vary mostly according to how large a group is writing the document and how well the group knows one another — that is, how close their views are at the start of the project. If diverse, the whole group will need to plan the document so that it can negotiate its goals. An individual may then draft the report, since it is very hard for a group to write together when individual word choices could be contested. In a diverse group, it is important for the group as a whole to respond to the draft and approve the final copy. Although no single person will author the text, the entire group will need to accept the text (or most of it).

In a large group, one member may start the process by drafting a "talking paper." The group may then request that the individual revise the draft substantially or the group may simply tinker with the draft so that it reflects their views. Here is the way one researcher described the co-authoring process that four individuals used to create an important memo proposing a new reading center.

> We came in and we worked ten to twelve hours a day, including Saturdays and Sundays — just constantly. . . . We fed each other ideas. Anne, who is a reading [specialist], would do some sort of writing draft, xerox it, and we'd all discuss it. We'd take what the panel of reading experts said and our ideas and through that — just that constant going back and forth — we came out with a fairly good research agenda for the new reading center.

Consultants often produce reports in this way. Alternatively, the group may plan the written product, and then an individual may draft and revise the paper for the group.

You will notice that the step most often completed by an individual is drafting. Rarely do committees actually compose reports in a large group — there are just too many choices to be negotiated. Only small teams of two or three people who know each other well and have worked together closely can draft easily together. Andrea Lunsford and Lisa Ede are a rare example of collaborative drafters. They write every word together. A more

THE FAR SIDE   By GARY LARSON

"So, then . . . Would that be 'us the people' or 'we the people?' "

common method of group drafting involves individuals writing sections of a piece and then passing each section around to all the authors for comment and revision. The five authors of *Women's Ways of Knowing* employed this approach. Each wrote a chapter and then they mailed the chapters around, each rewriting the chapters given to them until the entire book had been written and rewritten by all five authors. One of these authors, Jill Tarule, told me that as she retyped the chapters written by her colleagues, their words seemed to flow out from her fingertips — her thoughts and her collaborators' thoughts literally merged. This group did most of their work on separate college campuses, but their book was truly co-authored.

THE PROCESS OF WRITING WITH SEVERAL AUTHORS

The differences between writing alone and writing with several other authors involve management and authority. As a writer, you will go through the same steps of brainstorming, organizing ideas, drafting, and revising, but some or all of those steps will be done with other writers. Having already learned how to work with peer readers, you should have a sense of how to work with others efficiently. If you want to review the general guidelines for working in a group, reread Chapter 2. The following guidelines build on those recommendations for group work.

Managing a Collaborative Writing Project

In managing a group writing project, you need to consider how work is assigned, how the group will communicate, what timetable will be followed for the project, and how credit will be allocated. I think of these as the four C's of group writing: Control, Communication, Calendar, and Credit. For a group writing project to succeed, it must be important both to those writing it and those receiving it. The writers must know that their time is well spent.

Most groups larger than two need some kind of leader. In a business situation, the choice of a leader will probably be obvious — the senior member of the team or a person appointed by a supervisor. More informal groups will need to determine a leader. In small groups or collections of people who have worked together collaboratively for some time, the control of the group may be dispersed among its members. This management web will only work if those who are involved respect one another, trust the group to allocate responsibilities fairly, and can communicate easily and openly. Occasionally, a group may also be controlled by someone outside it — usually a supervisor. This is the structure in most educational situations where writers produce for a teacher. If the teacher establishes a timetable for the project, negotiates differences among members of the writing team, and evaluates individual contributions to the final project, then she is exercising control from outside the group. This kind of control works better for serial or compiled writing than for co-authored writing.

One of the most important things for a leader to establish is the writers' sense of control over what they write. Unless the project involves serial writing, the leader must be sure that writers have an opportunity to present their work to those who will later edit it and to respond to those editors' changes. If writers lose a sense of control over their texts, they will be less willing to contribute in the future and may upset the working atmosphere for the other writers.

If a group of people is accustomed to writing alone, they may need to adjust to an entirely new notion of authorship. Although co-authors need to have some control over their work, they will never have the kind of exclusive control individual writers have. Therefore, the pride that writers take in group work is different from the pride that they have in their individual work. Dissatisfied group members may feel that they are always compromising — that the final text is never exactly their ideal text. That reaction is normal — group work involves compromise. But this disadvantage is offset by the thoroughness and accuracy of a piece worked on by a group of individuals with multiple perspectives. Once people get accustomed to writing together, they no longer report feeling any difference between that process and writing alone. They are still proud of what they produce.

To resolve concerns about authorship, be sure that the group clearly allocates work in an equitable manner and determines from the start how public credit will be divided. The group members need to understand how important their contributions are. Keep the lines of communication open so that everyone has the sense of working in concert with everyone else. The group will also need to establish an open atmosphere so that if one member of the group feels unfairly burdened, that issue can be discussed freely. As I said in Chapter 2, the group will want to determine how to deal with such problems *before* they actually arise.

In addition to feeling that they are bearing a reasonable load and receiving appropriate credit, individual writers need to have a strong sense of the group as a whole. Allow time at the start of a project to develop that sense of common goals. Be sure from the start that the group recognizes the benefits of the diverse viewpoints that its members represent. The goal of group coherence is not to establish homogeneity so that everyone agrees on everything, but rather to discover how a collection of very different people can coordinate their efforts toward a common goal. If any member feels silenced by the group (not outvoted, but silenced), then the group is not taking full advantage of all its members' talents.

One of the most important documents in group writing is the calendar for the project. Coordinating individual efforts requires a strong sense of who must do what when. The calendar should be clear and yet flexible. If one member of the group misses a deadline by a day because of illness, the entire project should not collapse. Construct a calendar that includes a list of the end products that will be produced with due dates for each. Be sure to allow enough time for research and revision as well. Sometimes calendars look less like a list of dates than a research tree, showing how different individual research projects will dovetail. Here is a sample research tree that could also serve as the basis for a project calendar.

Project: To survey 1000 schools about their writing programs and compile the results in book form with introductory essays on programs in writing across the curriculum (WAC), writing centers (WC), and peer tutoring programs (PT).

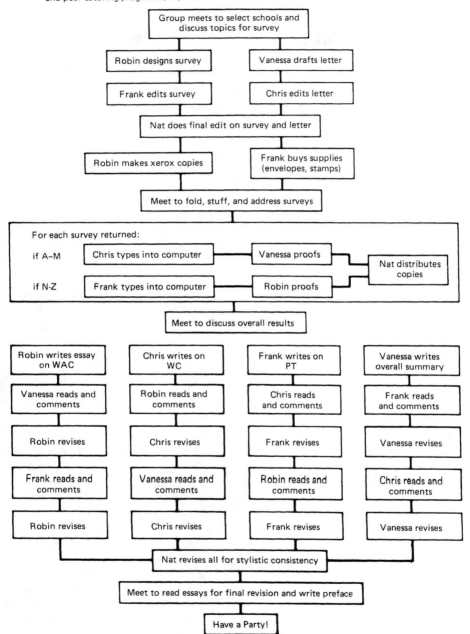

Even professional writers who have collaborated frequently report that group projects always seem to take longer than the writers anticipate. So a good rule of thumb is to estimate the time needed for each phase of the project and then increase that time by at least 50 percent. Some experienced collaborators say that you should double your expected time. I doubt if group projects really take more time than individual work, but they may seem to take longer because individuals have less control over their time when they work with a group. Also, the brainstorming that an individual may do while driving to work or eating lunch must be done in a group setting when everyone is obviously "at work."

Collaborative Brainstorming

Brainstorming is often done collaboratively because it draws directly on the different kinds of knowledge that various group members have. The goal of collaborative brainstorming, like that of individual brainstorming, is to accumulate ideas, not to sort or edit them — those stages come later. Therefore, as members of the group suggest ideas, other members should not judge or censor them. There is no need to correct one another.

Usually group brainstorming begins with a general discussion of goals. Sometimes those goals produce a series of questions that can guide the brainstorming session. Other times, the group will begin by exploring questions posed by an outsider — a client. Working through a list of the end products that the group must produce may also suggest questions for you to explore. As you participate in the group brainstorming, build on each other whenever possible. If someone suggests an idea and that triggers an idea in your head, toss it out. Some collaborative brainstorming sessions involve individuals role-playing (one suggesting ideas from the point of view of the public, another from the point of view of the environmentalists, another representing local industry). Sometimes these sessions read like a series of statements and counterstatements, as various sides of an issue are explored. If the group goes off on a tangent, allow that to happen until you know if the tangent is useful. If the tangent turns out to be irrelevant, the leader should pull the group back to the task at hand by saying something like, "Getting back to the problem of determining liability. . . ."

Another common procedure for brainstorming involves recording a group's ideas and then later allowing the group to brainstorm from that record. This process is often followed when groups cannot readily meet face to face. Allow a group to brainstorm about an idea and record the session in some way. Or, if every member of the group responds to a set of questions by writing to a single individual, that individual can transcribe the group's answers and send a report to all group members for comment. In this way, the group can reflect on the thoughts of its individual members.

Collaborative Organization and Planning

Most group processes involve individual members of the group organizing and planning on their own. Generally, groups can agree more easily on procedure and content than on presentation and style. But, in some processes, this stage is completed by the group. If you are part of a group that is trying to organize a piece of writing, be sure to define and order large blocks of material first. Deciding the order of individual sentences is even harder. Often large groups will subdivide into smaller groups in order to sketch out sections of a long report. I worked on a book with several other authors in which we each planned our own section (it was to be a compiled book), but then the group as a whole responded to our outlines. Seeing all the individual outlines at once helped to reveal overlapping concerns and gaps within the book.

In any case, when you are working with others to organize a large project, be sure that all individuals can see the evolving plan of the project so that they can feed into it. Use a large blackboard or a huge flip chart so that the group can work together. Even if the group is working on a short document (a statement of goals, for example), try to have everyone work from the same outline. It is hard to talk about relationships among sections of a report unless everyone is using the same terms and working from the same visual plan.

Collaborative Drafting

I do not recommend drafting anything in a group. Some pairs of people like Ede and Lunsford may succeed at group drafting, but group drafting is usually very frustrating. Sitting in a group and trying to shape ideas into prose is time consuming, and so usually the group allocates the draft to a single individual in the end. That individual can then write the draft and bring it back to the group for extension, response, and revision. It is much easier for a group to "draft" something if it is working in response to an individual's first version of the piece. A group can still feel responsible for a draft even if an individual provides them a first pull to work from. In fact, the final report may barely resemble the first draft, but the first draft still serves the purpose of providing a basic plan and some language to tinker with. As with writing papers alone, individuals who draft for a group should write more rather than less. Bring as much as possible to the group since it is much easier for a group to cut material than to generate it.

Collaborative Revision

Revising is often done collaboratively because it allows the entire group to take responsibility for the final product. Chapter 3 explained in some detail how an individual writer can benefit from feedback during the revising process. Groups can use peer review, too, by submitting their report to another group or to an individual for comment. This process can be especially helpful if the writers and the target audience for the paper are quite different. This is the theory behind focus groups used by advertising firms when they gather together consumers and ask them to respond to their latest product.

But groups may also revise their own work. Usually group revision begins with each member of the group reading a draft and making comments before coming together with others. If individuals can prioritize their comments, the meeting will go much more smoothly and individuals will be assured that their most important points get addressed. Work from large concerns to smaller ones, so that the group does not get mired in nit-picking about every word choice. Leave stylistic matters to an individual editor. If the group members insist that they need to approve the final style of the piece, have a single editor prepare the final draft and circulate it for comments. In this way, the group will not argue endlessly about grammatical fine points. The editor can just sort through and respond to the group's concerns.

Groups that have difficulty meeting face to face may pass a draft around, editing it as they go. If, for example, the final project has five sections, each drafted by an individual, then each of the five can send their work to one other person, in a round-robin fashion. Each writer can edit the draft he receives and pass it on to the next person and so on until the drafts are returned to the original authors. This procedure takes time, but it allows each writer to shape each part of the final project.

It is important in this process, as in all group revision, that the writers have an opportunity to respond to their editors. In book and periodical publishing, for example, authors submit their work to an editor who trims it or gives it a new shape to fit with the other submissions. Before publication, however, the writer has an opportunity to make any final changes in the piece. Respect the writer's need to see what will be published over or under her name. Individual writers must recognize, however, that they will need to compromise when working with a group.

REDEFINING AUTHORSHIP

Even though most writers collaborate to one degree or another during the writing process, the myth of the solitary writer remains strong. At the same time, the isolation of the writer is often cited as the most difficult aspect of writing. When a writer is alone, she must invent her own topics, act as her own audience, and try to create multiple perspectives to enrich her work. However, when a writer works with others, these problems diminish. Consequently, we need to redefine our notion of the author.

Our notion of the author has evolved in important ways since the Middle Ages when the author was seen as a copier. Then, truth was assumed to exist outside of individuals, and so individuals just copied various versions of it. Because there was no sense of individual truth, there was no need for a copyright law to protect individuals. The Renaissance, with its new sense of individualized truth as well as the invention of printing, gradually made copyright laws necessary. When publishing a text could yield the author a profit, he had something to protect. But copyright laws did not apply on an international scale until the twentieth century. So, now we protect the rights of individuals to their ideas. In fact, this protection has become so entrenched that we have trouble thinking about co-authorship — "Whose ideas are those, anyway?" we want to ask. As collaborative writing gains recognition and evolving technology makes data storage and sharing so much easier, the idea of the author will necessarily need to change.

One method of indicating primary authorship for a piece is to arrange the authors in order of descending importance. But some groups simply list their authors alphabetically. The problem with this procedure is that if two or more people co-author a piece, the first one cited (whether alphabetically or not) is assumed to be the primary author. As a result, the piece is usually catalogued under that author's name in card catalogs, indexes, bibliographies, and abstracts. The first author may or may not have played a primary role in the development of the piece. The practice of citing an article as "Adams, et al." is, therefore, questionable. Why should Adams get the bulk of the credit just because her name starts with "A"?

So, how do we define the author? The answer to that question will develop slowly over time. No one individual can redefine the author. Society will shape language to fit our changing needs and values. I look forward to the day when collaborative authorship will be common in all walks of life — including education — and will be recognized as a vital way for individuals to share ideas and work together.

Suggested Paper Topics

1. Study a local environmental problem from several different angles: legal, scientific, governmental, and so on. Write a full report with recommendations to the state's Interior Department.

2. Research the professional teams in a sport whose season is just beginning. Based on this research, predict the season's top three teams.

3. Identify a campus problem, and research possible solutions to it. Prepare a report with recommendations for the appropriate administrators.

4. Write an in-depth profile of Albania for a popular magazine like *Harper's*. Consider several broad aspects including Albania's history, economy, ethnic groups, political allegiances, and cultural life.

5. Investigate an unsolved murder and write up a group solution. Suggestions: Benjamin Nathan murder (1870), Charles Goodrich murder (1873), Richard Harrison Smith murder (1878), Jeanie Cramer's myste-

rious death (1881 — New Haven), Mrs. Henry H. Blise murder (1895), Emeline Reynolds murder (1898), Captain McDonald's family murder (1970). These subjects and others can be found in *Murder, Mischief, and Mayhem* (Urbana, IL: NCTE). All can be researched through the *New York Times*.

6. Compile a collection of articles with a group-authored introduction on the subject of date rape.

7. Write a collection of encyclopedia entries (for the same encyclopedia) on women artists in the twentieth century.

8. Study the safety or cost-effectiveness of the scientific labs on your campus. Prepare a report for the president of your college or university.

WORKS CITED AND FURTHER RESOURCES

Belenky, Mary, et al. *Woman's Ways of Knowing*. New York: Basic Books, 1986. (Includes student quoted on p. 85.)

Bouton, Clark, and Russell Y. Garth. *Learning in Groups*. San Francisco: Jossey Bass, 1983.

Bruffee, Kenneth. "Collaborative Learning and the Conversation of Mankind." *College English* 46 (November 1984), 635–652.

———. "Liberal Education and the Social Justification of Belief." *Liberal Education* 68 (1982), 95–114.

Ede, Lisa, and Andrea Lunsford. *Singular Texts/Plural Authors*. Carbondale: Southern Illinois University Press, 1987. (Includes comments by Albert Bernstein quoted on pp. 10 and 31, and the educational researchers quoted on pp. 31 and 94.)

Elbow, Peter. *Embracing Contraries*. New York: Oxford University Press, 1986.

———. *Writing with Power*. New York: Oxford University Press, 1981.

———. *Writing without Teachers*. New York: Oxford University Press, 1973.

Gere, Anne Ruggles. *Writing Groups: History, Theory, and Implications*. Carbondale: Southern Illinois University Press, 1987.

Hawkins, Thom. *Group Inquiry Techniques for Teaching Writing*. Urbana, IL: NCTE, 1976.

Hillocks, George. "Inquiry and the Composing Process: Theory and Research." *College English* 44 (1982), 659–673.

Holland, Norman. *Five Readers Reading*. New Haven, CT: Yale University Press, 1975.

Kohn, Alfie. *No Contest: The Case Against Competition*. Boston: Houghton Mifflin, 1986.

Langer, Ellen. "How Students Learn." *On Teaching and Learning* 2 (1987), 5–9.

Palmer, Parker. "Community, Conflict, and Ways of Knowing: Ways to Deepen Our Educational Agenda," *Change* 19 (September–October 1987), 20–25.

Ridland, Muriel. "Group Presentations of Poetry." In *Focus on Collaborative Learning*. Urbana, IL: NCTE, 1988. (Includes students quoted on pp. 29–30.)

Slavin, Robert. *Cooperative Learning*. New York: Longman, 1983.

Slavin, Robert, et al., eds. *Learning to Cooperate, Cooperating to Learn*. New York: Plenum, 1985.

Spear, Karen. *Sharing Writing*. Portsmouth, NH: Heinemann, 1988.

Trimbur, John. "Collaborative Learning and Teaching Writing." In Ben W. McClelland and Timothy R. Donovan, eds., *Perspectives on Research & Scholarship in Composition*. New York: MLA, 1985.

INDEX